Halifax

in action

by Jerry Scutts

illustrated by Don Greer

line drawings by Kevin Wornkey

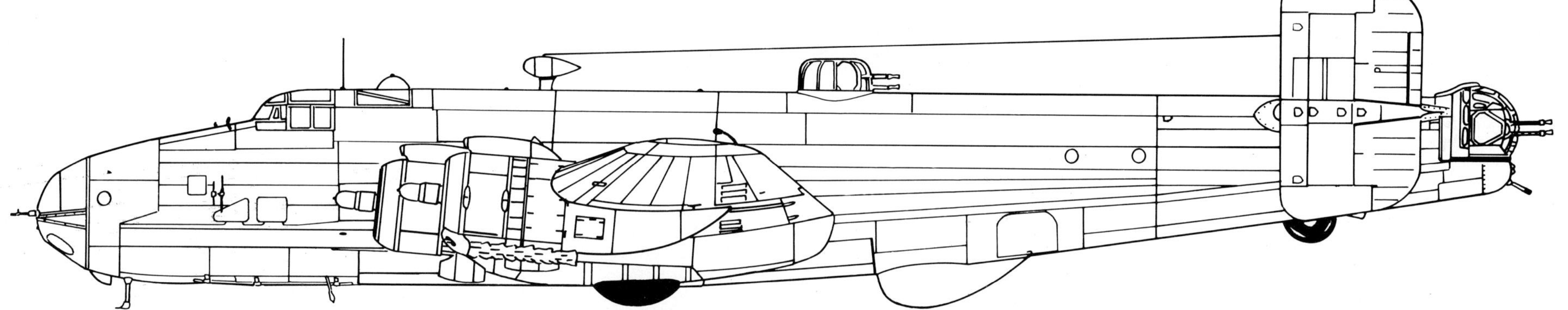

Aircraft Number 66

squadron/signal publications

"I'M EASY", a Halifax B Mk III of No 171 (Special Duties) Squadron, carrying out radio countermeasures with 100 Group.

Dedication:

This volume is respectfully dedicated to all those who went to war in Halifaxes.

Photo Credits

The author thanks the following individuals and organizations for their help in providing data and photographs for this volume:

Tony Fairburn	D. Taylor
A. H. Holmes	Dick Ward
Harry Holmes	Mick Wright
Howard Levy	Tom Goyer of Shorts
Ron Mackay	ECP Armees (ECPA)
Bruce Robertson	Flight International
Richard Riding, Editor, Aeroplane Monthly	Imperial War Museum
Chris Shores	Royal Canadian Air Force
	Rolls-Royce

This Halifax GR Mk II, believed to be JD178/V1 of 58 Squadron of Coastal Command during late 1943, carries the typical Coastal Command finish and a .5 inch Browning nose gun. (Sqdn Ldr Tony Fairburn)

Introduction

Anyone studying Royal Air Force Bomber Command's wartime effort to destroy the military and industrial might of the Third Reich will find that the Avro Lancaster was the cutting edge of that force. But, just as the US 8th Air Force had to face the Fortress versus Liberator question in its early months of combat — with the B-17 emerging the favorite — so too there developed a British command preference for the Lancaster over the other main RAF heavy bomber, the Handley Page Halifax. There were very practical reasons why this was so, but the net result was that the Halifax was operated in a variety of roles other than bombing, including maritime reconnaissance, troop carrier, transport and glider tug, and by so doing, its career was similar to that of the B-24.

To fulfill all these roles, the Halifax ran to about 22 versions based on eight main marks, three of which were powered by Rolls-Royce liquid cooled inline engines and five by Bristol Hercules air cooled radial engines. Between 1941 and 1945, Bomber Command Halifaxes dropped 227,610 tons of bombs on enemy targets and flew 75,532 sorties. They served as bombers not only in Europe but the Middle East, adistinction shared with no other British heavy bomber, and flew bomber support sorties in the Far East -- again, the only RAF four engined bomber to do so. Nearly 40 percent of all heavy bombers produced in Britain during the war were Halifaxes, an investment that gave the RAF a reliable, useful aircraft that served it well for more than a decade -- indeed, the Halifax outstripped all other British heavy bombers in duration and diversity of service.

The main problem with the Halifax — and the reason it was regarded as secondary to the Lancaster — was that it did not reach its full potential until the end of 1943, by which time it had already been in service for over two years, and by which time there were those who believed — Bomber Command chief Arthur Harris especially — that the RAF should have a heavy bomber force composed entirely of Lancasters.

Although a number of Halifax squadrons were converted to Lancasters, there were those who, understandably, did not always share 'Butch' Harris's view. Some men, particularly those who had flown both the Handley Page Halifax and the Avro Lancaster on operations, felt that the Halifax was the better aircraft. In particular, it was widely believed that the Halifax had superior 'survivability' — certainly there were numerous occasions when the Halifax was to demonstrate its ability to absorb heavy battle damage and still fly home. But then, this was equally true of the Lanc...

The initial design studies for the aircraft that became the Halifax were made in response to Air Ministry Specification B./15, issued in May 1935, calling for an all-metal mid-wing monoplane powered by either two air-cooled or liquid-cooled engines and intended eventually to replace the Whitley, subject of a 1934 specification. The Handley Page proposal, the HP 55, was rejected in favor of a Vickers proposal which was later to emerge as the Warwick which was destined to never become operational as a bomber.

New specifications for two bomber designs were issued in May 1936, calling for both twin-engined (B.13/36) and four-engined designs (B.12/36). Short Brothers, Supermarine and Handley Page tendered B.12/36 was to be met by the Short Stirling, the prototype of which flew for the first time on 14 May, 1939, but Supermarine's submission — the last of R. J. Mitchell's designs — was destroyed while still in the mock-up stage in 1940.

In response to the B.12/36 Avro submitted the Type 679, which became the Manchester. Having already investigated a twin-engined layout with the HP 55, Handley Page put forward the HP 56. The Air Ministry ordered two prototypes of the HP 56, to be powered by the new Rolls-Royce Vulture engines of 1,760 hp. Serial numbers L7244 and L7245 were allocated.

October 1939, the HP 57 prototype (L7244) a few weeks after completion, carries 'B' type fuselage roundels and what appears to be a top coat of washable camouflage paint, presumably in Dark Earth and Dark Green. Although the undersides appear dark, it is believed that they were in fact Yellow, with orthochromatic film reversing the color. The short lived Handley Page wing slots are fully extended. (Bruce Robertson)

A mock-up of the first HP 56 was completed before a conference warned Handley Page's chief test pilot Major James Cordes of possible delays in the Vulture engine program. The Rolls-Royce Vulture engine was basically two Kestrel engines mounted to a common crankshaft in an X configuration with four banks of cylinders. It was now suggested that the new bomber design might be adapted to take four smaller engines in the event that the Vulture's teething troubles proved incurable, and the choice lay between a quartet of Bristol Taurus radials or Rolls-Royce Merlin in lines. On 3 September, the Air Ministry contract was revised to confirm the installation of Merlin engines and the aircraft type number was changed to HP 57.

Production of the two prototype HP 57s began during the spring of 1938 under the design leadership of George Volkert at Handley Page's Cricklewood factory in North London. The first machine, L7244, was completed on 2 September 1939.

A conventional, well proportioned airplane, with a wingspan of 98ft 10in, the HP57 had a span marginally shorter than the Stirling or Lancaster (99ft, 1in, and 102ft, respectively). A mid-wing monoplane with flush-riveted stressed skin, the aircraft had box-section fuselage main frames with intermediate Z-section frames. A high strength front wing spar formed the center section, with T-section flanges under a sheet web forming the rear spar, the whole assembly bolting onto the fuselage sides.

Four Rolls-Royce Merlin X engines rated at 1,075 hp each at take off were mounted in Handley Page designed wide section nacelles which, although creating more drag than Rolls nacelles, would lessen modification time when Bristol Hercules radials were fitted later. Three-blade de Havilland metal propellers were used on the initial prototype, while the second prototype and service Halifaxes had compressed wooden blades.

The risk of enemy action damaging or destroying the prototype forced a move to RAF Bicester, Oxfordshire, for the first flight trials. The airfield at Cricklewood had long since been disposed of, and Handley Page's own airfield at Radlett in Hertfordshire was not considered large enough. Consequently L7244 was moved in sections by road to RAF Bicester where it was reassembled and flown for the first time on 25 October, 1939, with Major Cordes at the controls.

In May 1941, L7244 still carried its early camouflage paint, but shows evidence of repainting. Note the partially extended Handley Page wing slots on the outer wing panels and the short forward radio mast just behind the cockpit. (Robertson)

The second HP 57 prototype (L7245) in the standard 'new type' markings with yellow undersides. This was the first Halifax to carry armament. (Real Photos)

The first prototype had the nose and tail positions faired over but the second prototype (L7245) was fitted with a Boulton Paul type C two gun turret in the nose and a Boulton Paul type E four gun turret in the tail. Production type constant speed propellers with wooden blades were fitted and L7245 was flown from Radlett on 17 August 1940.

Developments

First Prototype L4244

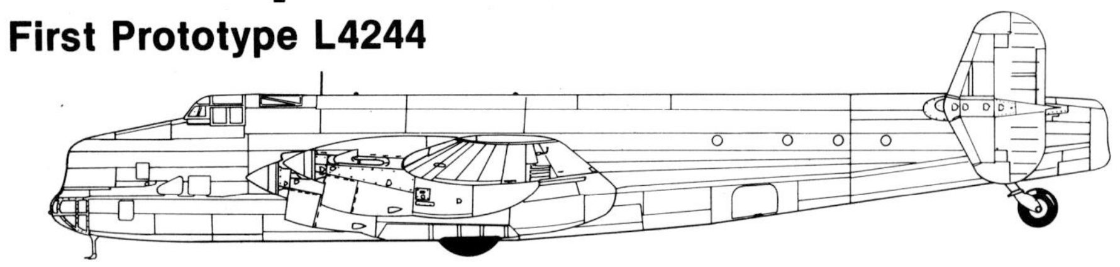

B Mk II Series 1a

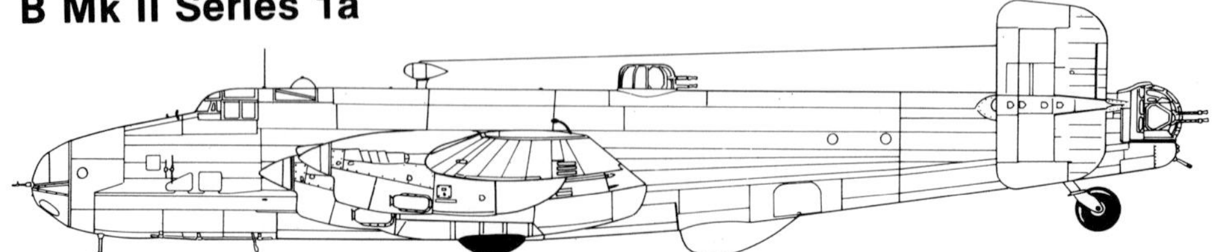

B Mk I Series 1

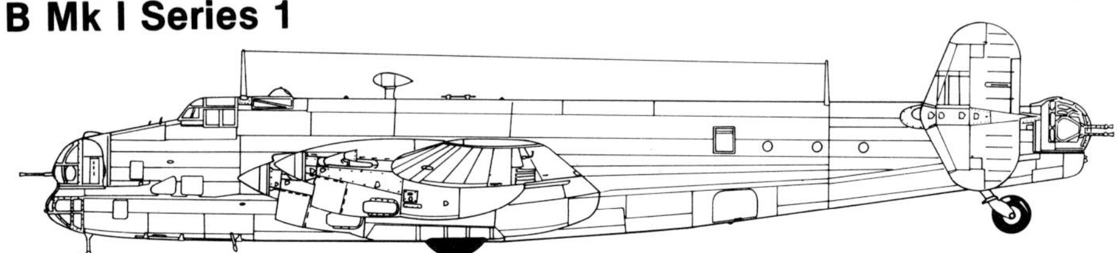

B MK III

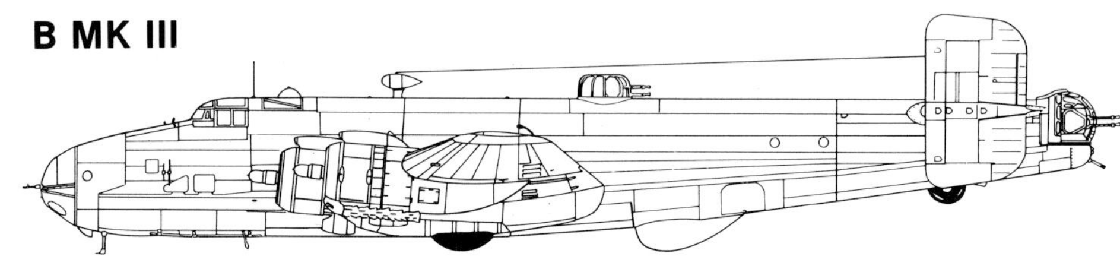

B Mk I Series 3

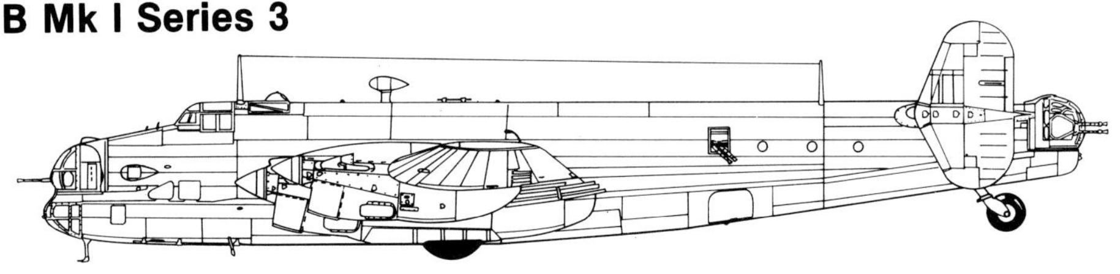

B Mk VI

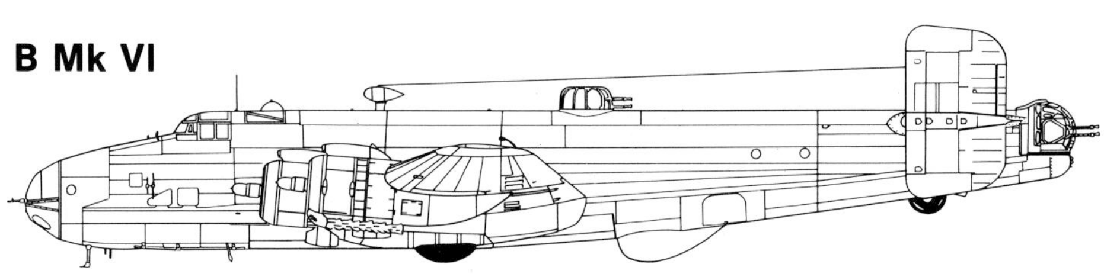

B Mk II Series 1

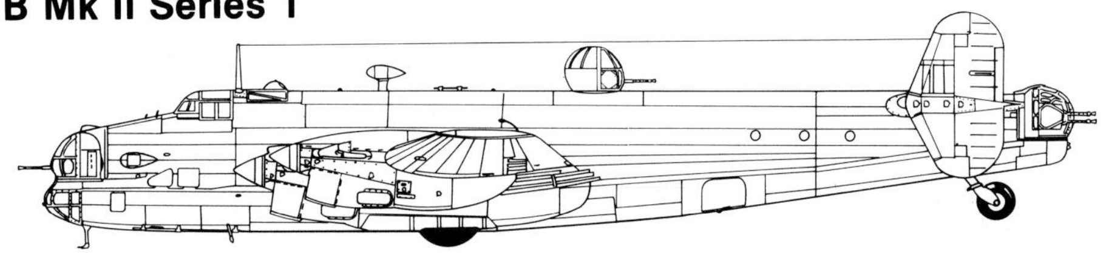

A Mk IX

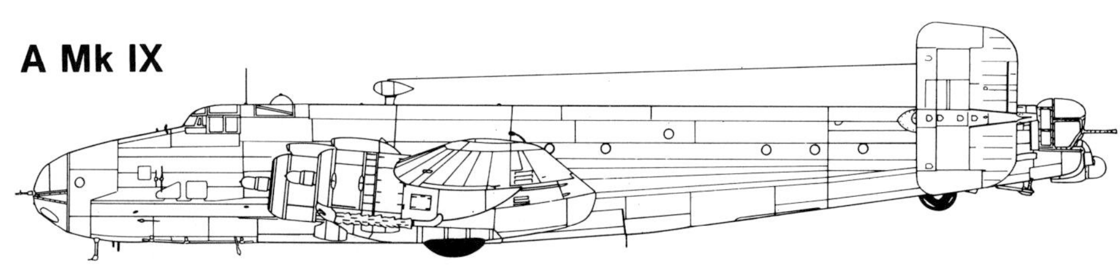

B Mk II Series 1 (Special)

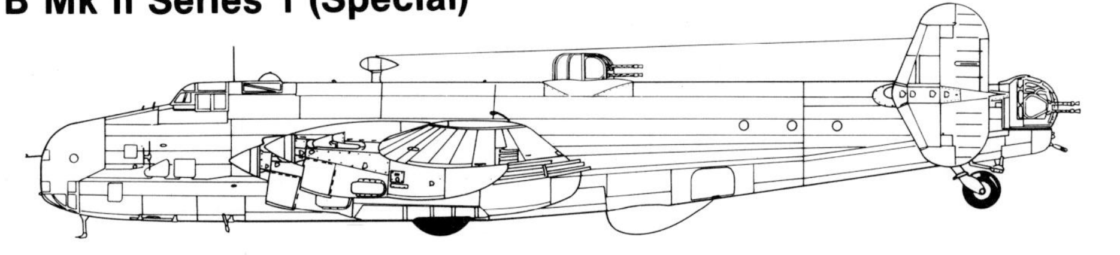

Halton

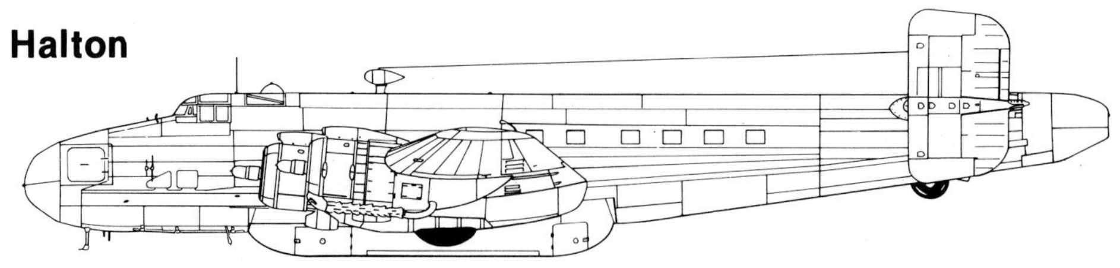

HALIFAX B MK I
Series 1 (HP 57)

A fully operational Halifax B Mk I, fuelled and armed, had an all-up weight of 55,000lbs, compared to 49,000lbs for the armed prototype. Fuel was distributed in eight main tanks in the wings between the engine nacelles, providing a normal total of 1,392 Imperial gallons. Two 80 gallon tanks could also be accommodated at each of two crew rest stations above the bomb bay for an additional 160 gallons (total 1,552 gallons) and up to three 230 gallon bomb bay tanks could be fitted for an absolute maximum fuel load of 2,242 gallons. Service ceiling at maximum weight was 18,000 feet and normal range with a crew of six was 1,700 miles. Maximum bomb load was 13,000 lbs, made up by various sizes of bombs in the fuselage bay and up to 500lbs in each of six inner wing cells, three per side.

Although all British wartime heavy bombers were strictly functional designs, the early Halifaxes were among the 'cleanest'. All early production Halifaxes had staggered waist or 'beam' gun positions which were covered by raise/lower windows. The port beam gun window was furthest forward, directly above the crew entry hatch which opened inward and upward, being hinged along its top edge. Up to two Vickers gas-operated (GO) guns could be used from each beam window, although their use was not standardized in Halifax squadrons. One thousand rounds of ammunition was provided for each gun in the nose turret and 6,800 rounds were provided for the four guns in the tail turret with 4,600 rounds in reserve.

The first production Halifax B Mk I (L9485) flew on 11 October 1940, and two days later was moved to Boscombe Down in Wiltshire for service testing where a nucleus of No 35

The fifth production Halifax (L9490), serving with No 35 Squadron, warms up on a snow covered field on 16 February 1941. This machine took part in the first Halifax raid of the war when seven of the heavies attacked the docks and shipping canal at La Havre on 10 March.

Halifax B Mk I Series 1 coded TL-P (L9503) of No 35 Squadron at Northolt on 21 July 1941, during an inspection by Winston Churchill. This machine was lost on the night of 15/16 September. (IWM)

Squadron personnel had been training on the first prototype, which had been temporarily fitted with dual controls. The second prototype was also used and when the unit moved, first to Leeming and then to Linton-on-Ouse in Yorkshire, L7244 and L7245 were retained until additional production aircraft arrived. No 35 Squadron's working up period lasted until the spring of 1941, by which time there were six experienced crews available. On the night of 10 March, the first Halifax operation of the war was carried out when six No 35 Squadron aircraft attacked Le Havre. All six machines returned to England safely, but one was mistakenly shot down over Surrey by an RAF fighter.

Handley Page's pre-war pioneering of split construction and unit assembly using photo lofting to produce identical component drawings was to serve the Halifax well. The original order for 100 aircraft had been increased to 500 under the RAF's 1938 expansion plans and the Air Ministry allocated additional production centers to meet it. Accordingly, English Electric at Preston, Lancashire, became the first of a network of sub-contractors known as the Halifax Group. The group would later embrace Fairey Aviation, Rootes Securities and the London Aircraft Production Group — which in turn comprised the London Passenger Transport Board and five firms which had previously built buses. At peak production the Halifax Group controlled 41 factories. The British automotive industry, like that of the United States, became a primary source of large manufacturing plants with a skilled work force that were retrained to fulfill unprecedentedly large orders for aircraft of all types.

In April of 1941 No 35 Squadron's 'C' Flight was expanded to provide the nucleus of a second Halifax squadron, No 76. Moving to Middleton St. George, County Durham, No 76 made its operational debut with Halifaxes on 12 June. And despite teething problems, especially with the hydraulic system, Halifax operations increased. On 24 July 1941, fifteen Halifaxes carried out a daylight raid on the Scharnhorst at La Pallice; five were lost and seven were damaged.

Most of the early Halifaxes carried a wavy demarcation between the Green and Brown upper surfaces and the Black lower surfaces. This wavy demarcation, which was also found on the engine nacelles, was short lived.

The four Merlin Xs, producing 1,075 hp at take off drove Rotol propellers of compressed wood. The Boulton Paul Type C nose turret mounted two .303 machine guns, while the BP E turret in the tail mounted four .303 guns.

Nose Turret

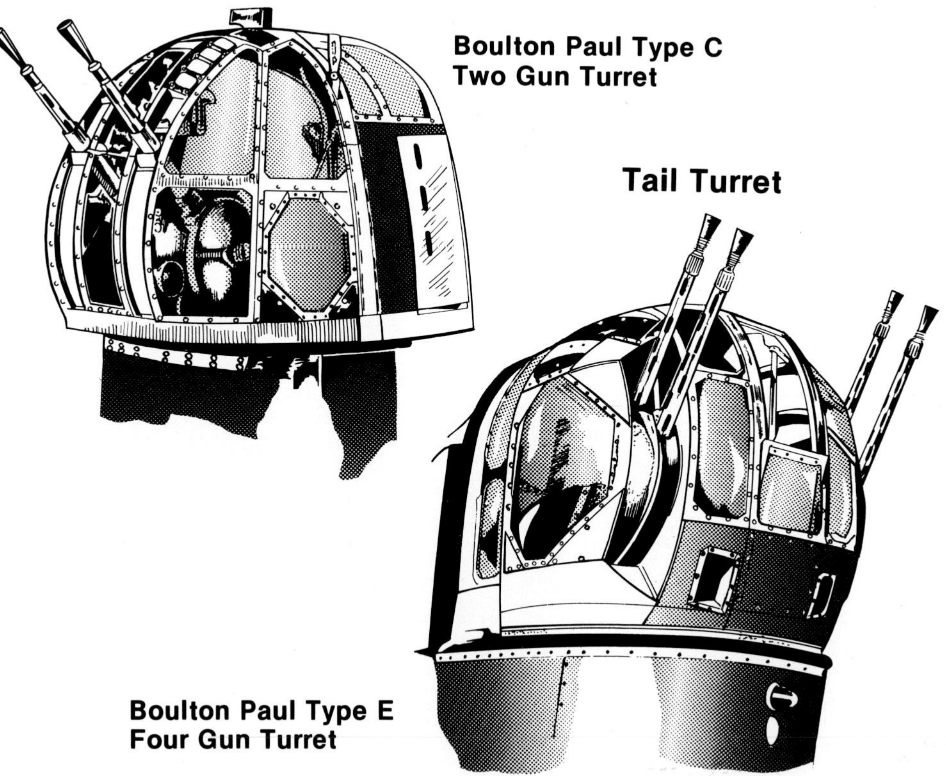

**Boulton Paul Type C
Two Gun Turret**

Tail Turret

**Boulton Paul Type E
Four Gun Turret**

Halifax B
MK I Series 2

Under the designation B Mk I Series 2 structural strengthening was carried out to permit an all up weight increase to 60,000 lbs. All twenty-five Series 2 aircraft (L9560 to L9584) had provision for twin Vickers beam guns, each weapon being fed by 96-round drum magazines. A rack holding ten drums was located at each gunner's station. The mass balance was moved to the upper surface of each aileron and teardrop observation blisters were added.

B Mk I Series 1

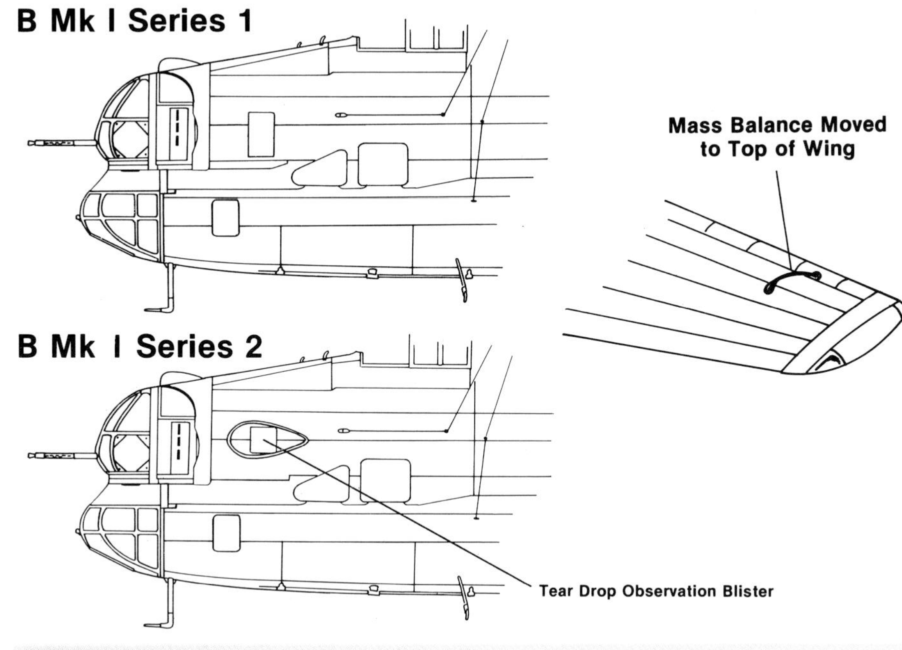

B Mk I Series 2

Halifax beam guns fired from staggered positions, the openings of which allowed it to become excruciatingly cold in the aircraft, especially at 20,000 ft. Each man wears an electrically heated flying suit, the leads, plugged into the aircraft's electrical system, can be seen running over the shoulder of the first gunner. Drums of ammunition are stacked in trays by each gunner. The overhead tracks carry ammunition to the rear turret. (Via M. Wright)

Returning from a mission against Italian targets, this B Mk I Series 2 is just about to touch down. The mass balances, which were moved to the upper wing surfaces, can just be seen above the outer wing panels.

Halifax B MK I Series 3

Deeper oil coolers with a distinctive lip on the underside of each cowling intake that extended back to the radiator flap were installed for the eventual accommodation of the new Merlin XX engines under the designation Series 3. Only nine Series 3 (L9600 to L9608) aircraft were built. The auto slots on the leading edge, which ran from the tips to the outer engine nacelles were deleted in favor of balloon cable cutters.

Fuel capacity was raised to 1,882 gallons as standard, a fifth 122 gallon tank being installed outboard of each outer engine nacelle. Provision for the fuselage rest station tanks was consequently dispensed with, although the extra bomb bay tanks could still be fitted as needed. In order to jettison fuel if an emergency landing had to be made just after take off three fuel jettison pipes were installed on the rear lower surfaces of each wing between the engine nacelles. These jettison pipes were flexible as they ran across the flaps so the flaps could operate freely. A third electrical generator was also added to the port outer engine. The last Halifax Mk I Series 3 (L9608), was the aircraft used in the official naming ceremony by Lady Halifax at Radlett on 12 September, 1941.

The last of the Mk I series 3 (L9608) served as the ceremonial Halifax aircraft when Viscountess Halifax christened the new four engined bomber.

Oil Cooler Intake

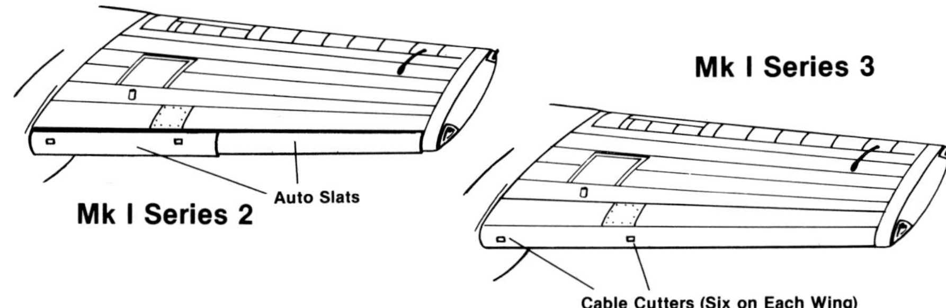

The nine B Mk I Series 3s introduced features carried over to the Mk II, including the deeper oil cooler lip on the engine nacelle undersides. The second machine of the production batch, L9601, served with No 76 and No 78 Squadrons. (Flight International)

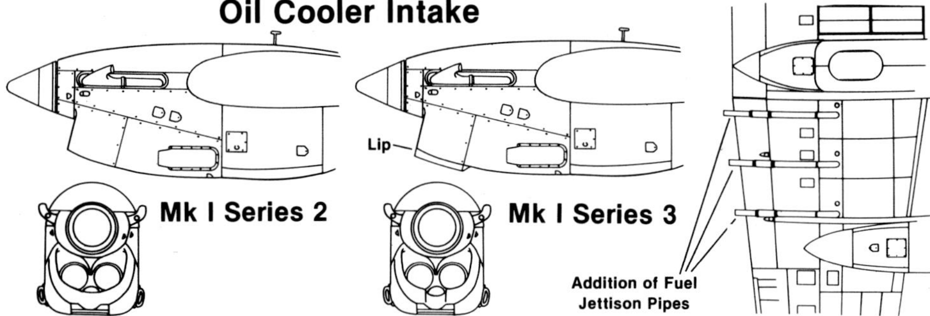

Halifax B MK II Series 1 (HP 59)

Installed in a test aircraft (L9519), the 1,280 hp Merlin XX engines demonstrated the potential for a marked increase in Halifax performance. Major Cordes flew L9515, which became the prototype Mk II, from Radlett on 3 July 1941, and English Electric delivered the first production example (V9976) on 15 August. The first few aircraft did not have the bulbous Boulton Paul C dorsal turret (similar to that fitted to British Lockheed Hudsons) and retained beam guns. Later in the production run turret equipped aircraft had the beam guns and the rear fuselage radio mast removed, and aerial location points were added to the fins.

No 35 Squadron was again the first recipient of the new Halifax, with two aircraft being taken on strength during late October. In December No 10 Squadron converted from Whitleys to Halifax Mk IIs, becoming the third Halifax unit in No 4 Group.

Having helped force the Scharnhorst to move to Brest in June, Halifaxes were part of a mixed force that attacked the ship in that port on 18 December. All three squadrons participated, with their targets including the battleship Gneisenau. One Halifax was lost and some damage was done to the German ships. Halifaxes made up the entire force of sixteen aircraft sent against the same targets on the 30th, but this time fighters and flak claimed three bombers. The inconclusive results and the losses sustained during these and previous daylight attacks resulted in Bomber Command switching to night raids almost exclusively until 1944.

But the end of daylight sorties did not see the finish of heavy bomber sorties against German capital ships. On the night of 28/29 January 1942, Halifaxes initiated the massive British effort to destroy the battleship Tirpitz. Detachments from No 10 and 76 Squadrons flew an abortive operation, only one Halifax actually locating the target.

More conventional bomber targets were struck by Halifaxes in the early weeks of 1942, Air Marshal Harris taking over as Commander-in-Chief of Bomber Command in late February. Almost immediately there was a portent of things to come. On the night of 3 March Halifaxes contributed to a very successful raid on the Renault works at Billancourt near Paris.

The Tirpitz was again bombed by Halifaxes on the night of 301 March, when 34 aircraft used conventional bombs and 1,000lb mines. Six aircraft failed to return and there was no damage done to the ship. In April, a Halifax of No 76 Squadron dropped the first 8,000lb bomb ever used by Bomber Command, on Essen. That month also saw the delayed operational debut of the next Halifax squadron, No 102 at Dalton, Yorks. No 102 had received its first Halifaxes the previous December but had been held back from operations pending delivery of aircraft fitted with the navigational aid Gee. Late April also recorded the last Halifax attacks on the Tirpitz — on the night of the 27/28th, with the loss four aircraft* (again for no damage to the ship). The last Halifax raid on Tirpitz took place on the 28/29th of April and once again No 35 Squadron suffered casualties without damaging the ship. Two aircraft failed to return.

Two more squadrons, No 78 and 405 (RCAF), converted to Halifax Mk IIs before the historic 1,000 bomber raid on Cologne on the night of 30/31 May. The raid caused tremendous damage to the city and thereby reprieved Harris's bomber force from being broken up and redistributed throughout other RAF commands. At last the bombers had proven that they were capable of devastating a target. There were 118 Halifaxes over Cologne that night, the aircraft being drawn from all six first line squadrons, and 1652 Heavy Conversion Unit.

***Among those lost was W1048 of No 35 Squadron. This was the machine that, having crash landed on the frozen surface of Lake Hoklingen after the attack, was raised from the lake bed in 1973. Virtually intact, 'S for Sugar' now rests in the RAF Museum, Hendon, the only survivor of the entire Halifax line on public display.**

By the late summer of 1942 there were five Halifax squadrons in No 4 Group, one in No 1 Group (No 103) and one in No 6 Group (No 405). No 103 Squadron had converted to Lancasters in October, by which time the original Halifax unit, No 35, had been transferred to the new Path Finder Force (PFF). Being selected as one of the five squadrons to form the nucleus of No 8 (PFF) Group was a tribute to the skill and experience No 35 Squadron had gained during the eighteen months of operations in Halifaxes — particularly since the record of the aircraft itself had been somewhat disappointing.

The Halifax's most serious problem, that of rudder stalling, persisted. It had shown up in early Boscombe Down tests, and in the summer of 1942 A&AEE began a further series of investigations aimed at curing it. Among a number of Mk Is and IIs used for flight tests was W7919, a standard service Mk II belonging to No 102 Squadron. The fatal crash of this machine on 4 February 1943, revealed the worst effect of the rudder design and finally confirmed that overbalancing was certainly the cause of some crashes. Investigation of the wreckage found that the top half of one rudder had been torn off in flight.

Modification had already been made to the tail assembly by Mod 413, the addition of a bulbous rudder leading edge, and a restricter on the balance tab. It had been assumed that the Halifax only had a tendency to overbalance under certain flight conditions, but

Powered by 1,280 hp Merlin XX engines this uncoded Halifax B Mk II is on a flight test. The emergency fuel jettison pipes are silhouetted against the overcast. Normally taking off in an overload (for landing) condition, the jettisoning of fuel became critical if an emergency landing was to be made just after take off. (Aeroplane)

(Above) No. 10 Squadron Halifax IIs in flight. The sister aircraft of BB194 shows to advantage the aileron mass balance, the fuel jettison pipes on the bottom of the flap, and the breather/filler pipes for the outboard wing tanks. There were six breather/filler pipes on the early marks of Halifax. BB194 is an early Mk II without the bulbous Boulton Paul C mid upper turret. (IWM)

A Halifax B II ZA-E (BB194) of No 10 Squadron undergoing extensive engine maintenance. The engine cowlings have been removed exposing the oil coolers. As in all air forces the ground crewmen were the unsung heroes, working long and hard to keep their charges in the air. (A. H. Holmes)

the crash of W7917 proved that at speeds of 120 mph or less, any violent operation of the rudders, coupled with sideslipping, could throw the aircraft into an uncontrollable spin.

Boscombe Down test pilots found that the Halifax could easily be induced to spin, during which it lost some 4,000 feet of altitude — it can be imagined what happened when a damaged aircraft, particularly one with two engines out on one side, tried a cross-wind landing. Working his rudders to correct the inevitable swing, a pilot could easily create a stall condition. Worse still, some Halifaxes were undoubtedly lost on operations when their pilots executed the standard evasive 'corkscrew' maneuver to shake off a night fighter, using full rudder to make the necessary turns.

An interim 'fix' was to reduce rudder travel by a restricter fitted to the rudder bar to limit movement of the rudder to twelve rather than the standard twenty degrees. The only other safety measure that could be made quickly was to stress the problem to aircrews. And while these measures did reduce losses through accidents, the real answer was to increase the size of the vertical tail surfaces.

But all problems were not confined to the Halifax's tail unit; when Boscombe Down tested the aircraft for exhaust flame-damping properties, engine performance and general reliability for service use, the early Mk IIs were found wanting in all respects. Although not unique in suffering a weight penalty from additional operational equipment, examples of the Mk II were also found by A&AEE to show a low standard of workmanship in manufacture, aggravated by poor servicing. In one test, using DG221 of No 78 Squadron, part of the report stated that the aircraft had such a poor take off performance and that 'any slight faltering on the part of the pilot would be disastrous.'

Answering an urgent call for more heavy bombers to boost the Liberator and Wellington force engaged in attacking Axis ports and supply lines in the Mediterranean, No 10 and 76 Squadrons despatched 30 Halifax IIs to Aqir, Palestine, in July of 1942. On arrival these Bomber Command elements were combined with other detachments as 249 Wing and flew their first operation on the night of 1/2 July, when a single No 10 Squadron Halifax bombed Tobruk.

Tobruk was to remain a priority target for many months, but by September the wing was ranging as far as Crete. On 6 September both squadron elements were combined to form No 462 Squadron (RAAF). A hectic pace of operations was maintained in the face of technical problems with the Halifaxes, not the least of which was engine trouble. When the battle of El Alamein began on 23 October 1942, No 462 began direct support of Allied ground forces, in which role it increasingly engaged in ground strafing, a unique role for the four engined Halifax. Some operations of this nature were pressed home from as little as 1,200 feet!

The squadron led a nomadic existence in the desert, there being few permanent servicing facilities. Ground crews performed wonders of improvisation to keep their charges in the air. But by January, 1943, the pace was telling and Halifax sorties were curtailed almost completely awaiting the arrival of fresh aircraft. At the same time, permission was received to remove front and dorsal turrets and make local modifications, the result being that the desert B IIs looked similar to their European counterparts. Later, some B II Specials were operated by No. 462.

In May a second Mediterranean bomber squadron, No 178, received some B IIs to support its B-24 Liberator operations. Since the Halifax crews had located their targets by dead reckoning and astro navigation, it was decided that the Australian squadron would henceforth become a pathfinder force for the Wellington and Liberator main force. By the end of September, 1943, No 178 had passed its Halifaxes to No 462 and these aircraft, fitted with the much more reliable Merlin 22s, were quickly pressed into service.

In January of 1944, No 462 was given the job of acting as pathfinders for the entire central Mediterranean bomber force and the first Gee and H2S equipped B II Series Ia Halifaxes were received. For the invasion of Sicily, both No 178 and 462 Squadrons were temporarily placed under the operational control of IX Bomber Command, USAAF.

On 3 March 1944, No 462 was renumbered No 614 Squadron at Celone, Italy, and in August, the squadron marked Ploesti for main force bombers. Toward the end of 1944 it was slated to re-equip with Liberators, but these were slow in coming and No 614's last Halifax sorties were flown on 3 March, 1945.

Nimble feminine fingers check the bomb aimer's panel in the nose of a Halifax. At the top can be seen the instrument panel bridge with throttle controls on the extreme left.

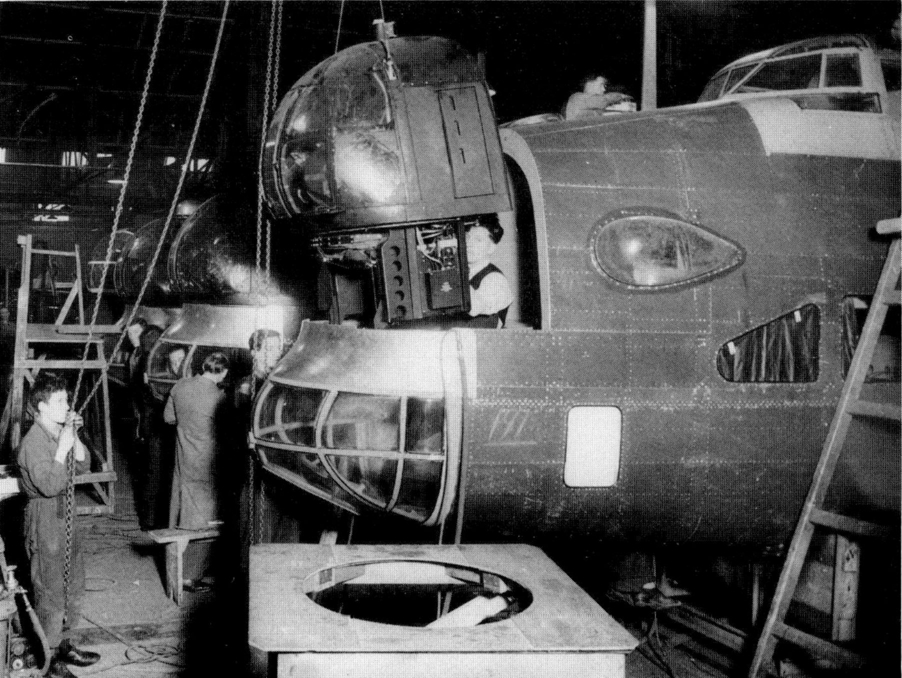

Halifax front fuselages on the production line. Apart from guns and ammunition boxes, the Boulton Paul C type nose turret went in complete.

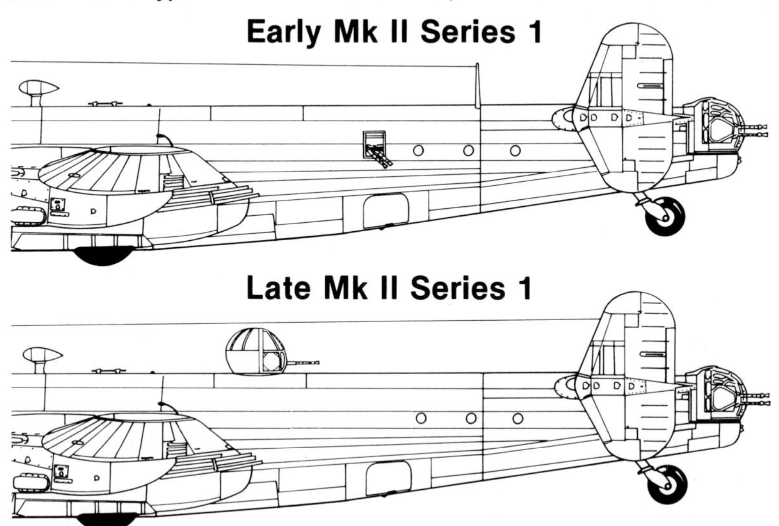

Early Mk II Series 1

Late Mk II Series 1

When the bulbous Boulton Paul C dorsal turret, armed with a pair of .303 machine guns, was installed on later B Mk II Series 1 aircraft, the four beam guns were deleted. The rear antenna mast was also removed and aerial attachment points added to the fins.

The turret's ammunition boxes protruded into the bomb aimer's compartment on either side of the bomb aimer. (IWM)

June '42 and a Halifax Mk II is prepared for the coming night's operation by both machine and muscle power of the armorers. (Aeroplane)

Aid from the USA to Britain in the early war years wasn't always in the form of weapons. Cash donations bought this YMCA tea car for an RCAF Halifax base. One of the six per wing cable cutters can be seen in the juncture of the engine nacelle and the leading edge of the wing. (Aeroplane)

Comparison of camouflage treatment on ZA D (R9376) of No 10 Squadron and TL P (W7676) of No 35 Squadron demonstrates the basic differences between the early wavy demarcation line and the later straight demarcation line. Also of interest is that ZA D still retains the rear aerial mast even though it is armed with a mid upper turret. (Aeroplane and R. L. Ward)

Exhaust Shroud

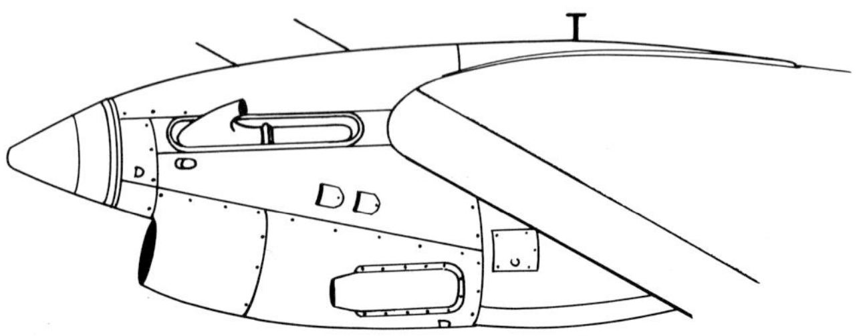

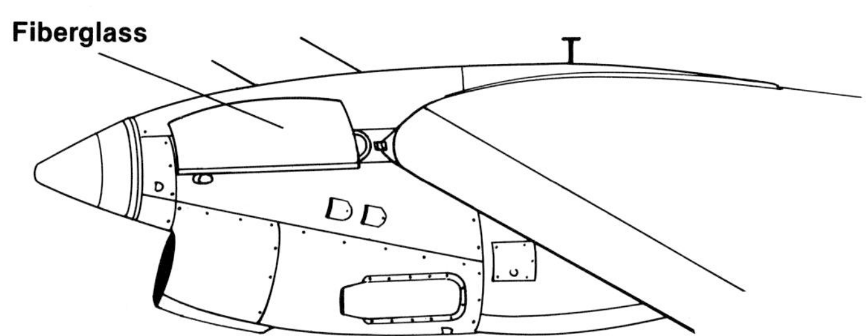

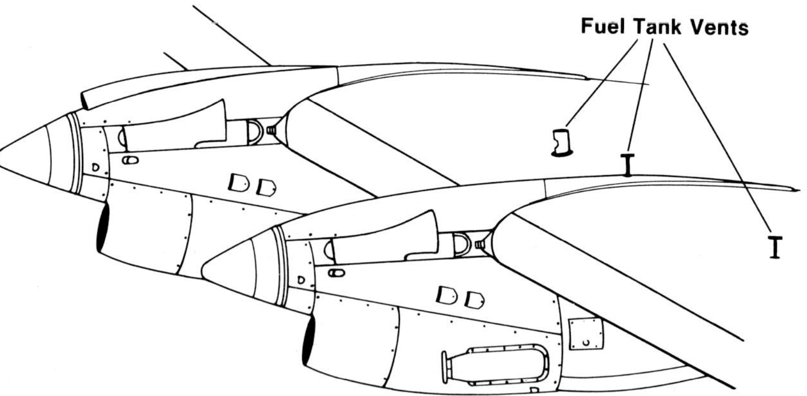

An early B Mk II attacking German battleships at Brest in December of 1941, a Halifax releases 500lb bombs from its wing bays. The beam guns can just be seen on either side of the fuselage. (IWM)

Engine check. The early Merlins required a good deal of preventive maintenance. (Aeroplane)

Topping off the tanks of a No 76 Squadron Halifax. (Aeroplane)

The Halifax cockpit changed little throughout the aircraft's service life, although the window below the windscreen seen in this view was deleted. The massive but easily handled throttle levers are much in evidence as are the propeller speed control levers below them, and mixture and supercharger levers in the fully down position at the bottom of the pedestal. The bright metal bow tie affair in the center of the control column grip is the wheel brake. (R. L. Ward)

This Mk II Series 1 (W1245) of No 78 Squadron, failed to return from a raid on Mainz on 12 August 1942. (R. L. Ward)

This Halifax B Mk II (W1170) in company with six other aircraft of No 10 Squadron left England on 6 July 1942, for the Middle East in response to a call for more heavy bombers in that theater, but went temporarily unserviceable at Gibraltar before rejoining the squadron. Seven missions are chalked up here and the European theater squadron codes ZA have been overpainted, leaving only the individual letter identifications, as required in the MTO. (IWM)

This October 1942 scene is also believed to have been at Driffield, home of No 405 Squadron. Once again, engine attention is much in evidence. This B Mk II does not have the teardrop observation blister just behind the nose turret. (RCAF)

The Driffield crew bus drops Q Queenie's crew at dispersal before a night raid by No 405 Squadron, the first Canadian bomber squadron formed overseas. Q Queenie was serialed W7703. The long winter nights allowed deep penetration into Germany, however the short days of summer, when it stayed light until nine or ten o'clock at night and got light at four or five o'clock in the morning, allowed only a shallow penetration of the Reich.(IWM)

B Mk II Series 1

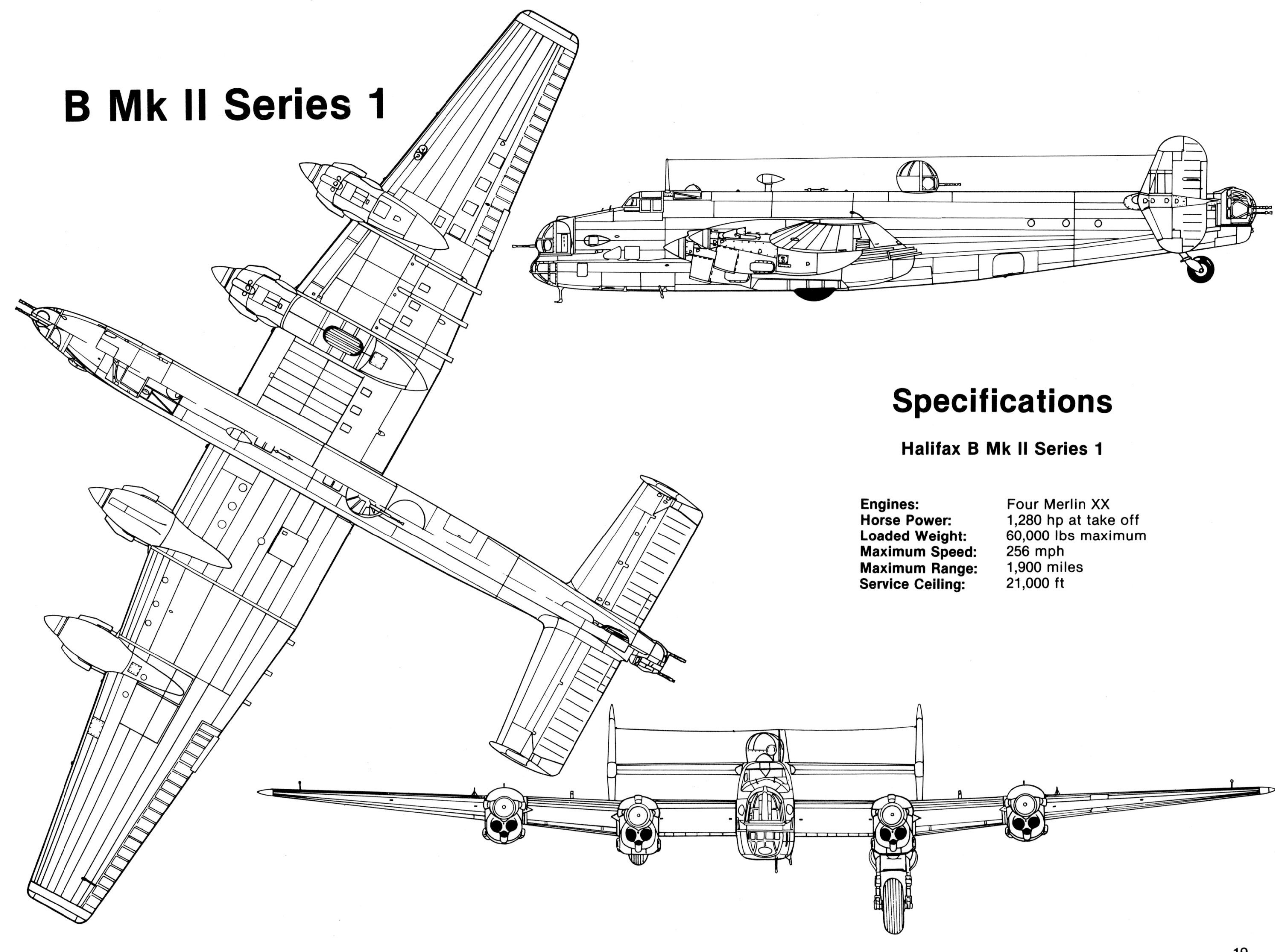

Specifications

Halifax B Mk II Series 1

Engines:	Four Merlin XX
Horse Power:	1,280 hp at take off
Loaded Weight:	60,000 lbs maximum
Maximum Speed:	256 mph
Maximum Range:	1,900 miles
Service Ceiling:	21,000 ft

W7710 of No 405 Squadron highlights some of the 'lumps and bumps' that had to go in order to improve the Halifax's performance. (RCAF)

Halifax B MK II
Series 1 (Special)

Boscombe Down initiated a general 'clean-up' program for the Halifaxes it had under test, aimed primarily at weight-savings. The front turret was removed and the top half of the nose section was covered by a fairing. Many aircraft also lost their mid-upper turret, thereby saving a total weight of 1,450lbs, the result being that the Halifax gained sixteen mph in top speed, equal to a further savings of 840lbs of fuel and oil over a range of 1,800 miles. The result was designated the B Mk II Series 1 (Special).

The first Halifaxes without nose turrets were used by Special Duties (SD) Squadrons, but unit modified aircraft quickly began to appear in No 4 Group. The nose fairing, officially Mod 398, was variously known as the 'Tollerton' after Tollerton Aircraft Services, which made the first conversion; 'Tempsford' after the base from which the modified aircraft of No 138(SD) Squadron first operated); and the 'Z-Fairing' from the additional fuselage framing required to support the sheet metal covering. Differing slightly in outline shape from the early conversions, 'factory' Mk II nose fairings invariably had two horizontal windows above the bomb aimer's clear panels to restore some of the lost forward vision.

Because of a reduced need for frontal defense the loss of the front turret gave little cause for concern among most of the Halifax crews, who welcomed the resultant performance increase. Some crews, however, balked at losing the dorsal turret as well and there was much discussion on the need for some form of defense for the vulnerable undersides of the aircraft. The latter problem would never be completely solved, although the first production B Mk I had tested two different twin-gun ventral turrets, the FN 64 and Boulton Paul K Mk I.

An easier solution was to double the number of dorsal turret guns and Halifax IIs began to receive the excellent four gun Boulton Paul A Mk VIII type turret. Light and efficient, this turret weighed only 586lbs complete and incorporated 7.5lbs of 12mm armor plate. Each gun had 550 rounds.

In this interim development period, individual Halifaxes differed to quite a degree and flew operations with full or partial weight saving modifications; the early Mk VIII turrets were set on a raised fairing containing the interrupter gear to meet an Air Staff requirement for 10 degrees depression. The added drag of the fairing subsequently led to the new turret being set flush with the fuselage top on a shallow metal skirt.

Full weight savings extended to removal of the fuel jettison pipes, carburetor ice guards for the air intakes, wing leading edge balloon cable cutters, and even the elimination of the Kilfrost anti-icing paste on control surface leading edges. The rough finish RDM2 black paint was discontinued. Painted over standard 'night' paint, RDM2 clipped up to five mph off the aircraft's top speed.

Other items removed included the fairing in front of the flare chute, the handrail on top of the fuselage aft of the D loop fairing and the rear radio mast. Fuselage and wing panel joints were sealed and attention was paid to improving engine performance. A first step was to discontinue use of the large asbestos tunnel shrouds which, it was found, created turbulence over the inboard engine nacelles and caused vibration at the wing trailing edge. Radiator overheating was cured by cropping the flaps and increasing the outlet area, and finally, investigations were made into a better method of flame damping without adversely affecting the exhaust system.

B Mk II (Specials) were introduced to operational squadrons in the autumn of 1942, at a time when Bomber Command's target list still included locations in Italy as well as France and Germany. Turin and Genoa were consequently bombed by Halifaxes before the early months of 1943 saw a concerted effort against German cities. Diversions from what Harris saw as the main objective of his force nevertheless continued on a reduced scale, pressed as the C-in-C was from various quarters eager to have more specialized targets attacked. U-boat pens had, for example, long been seen as primary heavy bomber targets and although raids undoubtedly caused widespread destruction in the ports, the huge con-

Detail of the Z-fairing nose of the MK II Series 1 (Special) with the factory fitted windows to help the straight-ahead view. The aircraft is DT792 of No 19 Squadron (R.L. Ward)

Nose Development

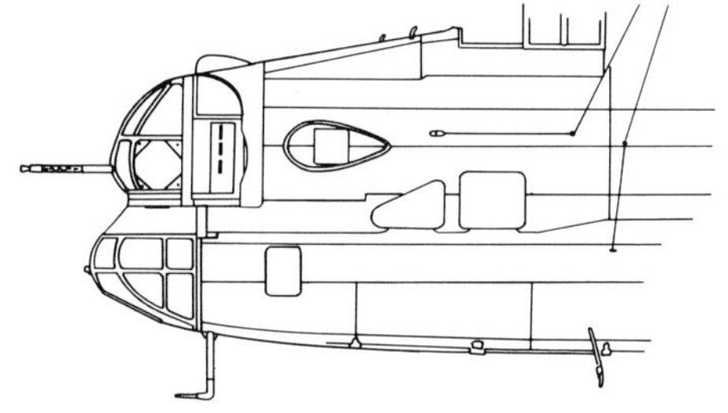

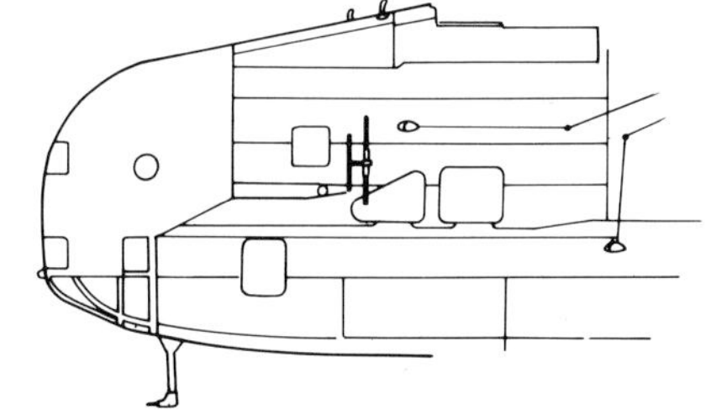

B Mk II Series 1

B Mk II Series 1 (Special)

crete pens remained invulnerable to the bombs then in use.

But by early 1943, Harris was able to hit Berlin for the first time since the German capital had been attacked on a small scale in 1941. On the night of 16/17 January, 201 Halifaxes and Lancasters dumped their loads of HE and incendiaries in the southern part of the city and lost but one Lanc. By contrast, a follow-up raid the next night resulted in the loss of 22 bombers; and while the squadrons then had little defense against radar predicted flak and cannon armed night fighters, 30/31 January saw the introduction of a significant new aid to target location, H2S radar.

The target that night was Hamburg; six No 35 Squadron Halifaxes and seven Stirlings of No 7 Squadron set out to mark the city for the main force. In the event only two Halifaxes and four Stirlings were able to carry out their task, the early H2S sets being prone to failure. But radar marking of Cologne, Hamburg and Turin quickly followed, proving beyond doubt the value of the new device. Production of the sets was slow at first and it was not until the autumn of 1943 that the three RAF heavies operated in any numbers with the distinctive ventral cupola protecting the radar scanner.

The extent of the Halifax 'clean-up' program is well illustrated by this view of 'Haig's for Victory' (BB324), which carries markings of four sorties. The nose turret has been replaced by a Z fairing, the spine handrail has been removed, and the fuel vents normally found on the rear of each outboard engine nacelle have been deleted. Initially issued to No 76 Squadron, BB324 passed to No 10 Squadron and failed to return from a raid on Mulheim on 23 June 1943. (Aeroplane)

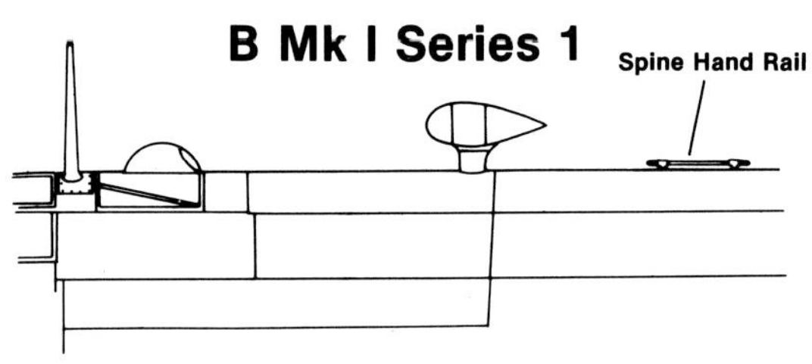

B Mk I Series 1

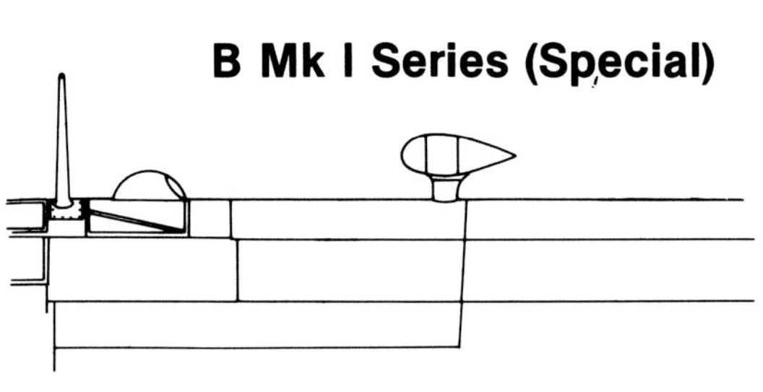

B Mk I Series (Special)

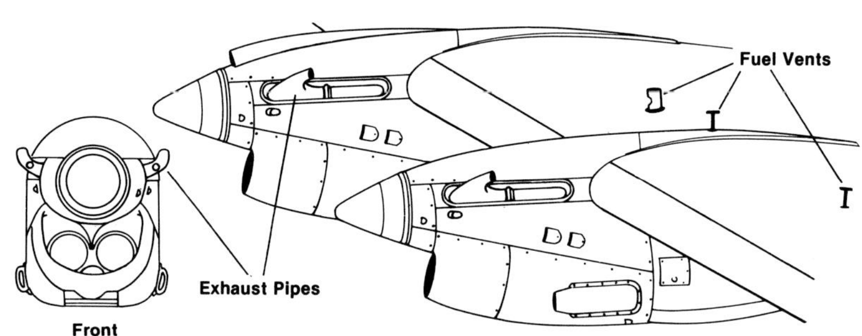

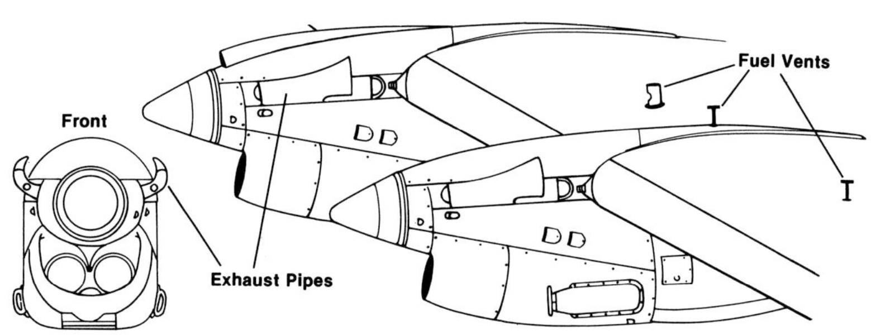

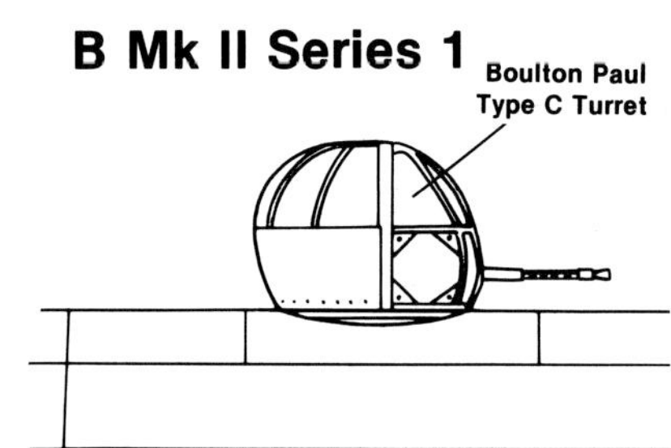

B Mk II Series 1

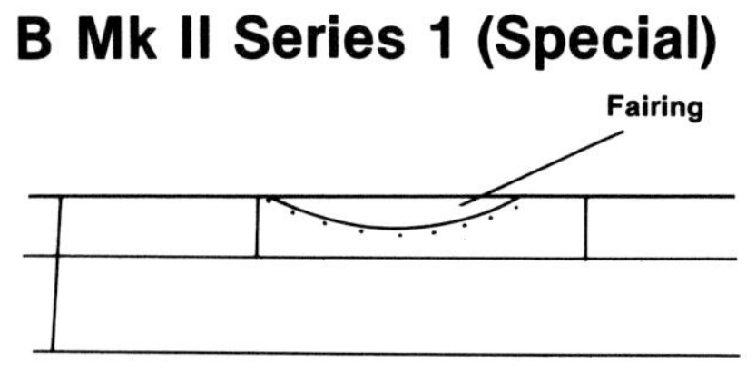

B Mk II Series 1 (Special)

Interesting comparison of 'local' and factory modifications to create B II Series 1 (Specials) for Middle Eastern service. The unmarked machine (above) at Fayid, Egypt, on 4 March 1943, retains the fairing for the turret controls on the top of the nose — and indeed appears to have the turret retained under the black paint, while BB325 (Below), also at Fayid, on 17 April 1943, has a standard factory installed Z fairing. Both aircraft are believed to have been from No 462 Squadron. (Howard Levy)

The low level beat up of Elvington by No 77 Squadron's B II Series I (Special) (JB911) in July of 1943, delights the troops, who seem to be encouraging a following Halifax to do the same. Their perch is KN-M which, like KN-X, has a transparent observation bubble on the fuselage underside and the raised decking to the Boulton Paul four gun turret. (IWM)

Mid Upper Turret and Removal Fairing

**Boulton Paul
A Mk VII Turret**

'Maid of the Mountains' had scaled the heights forty times when photographed in the Middle East in 1944. The Light Stone and Dark Earth camouflage demarcation line on the nose varied considerably on B II Specials. (R. L. Ward)

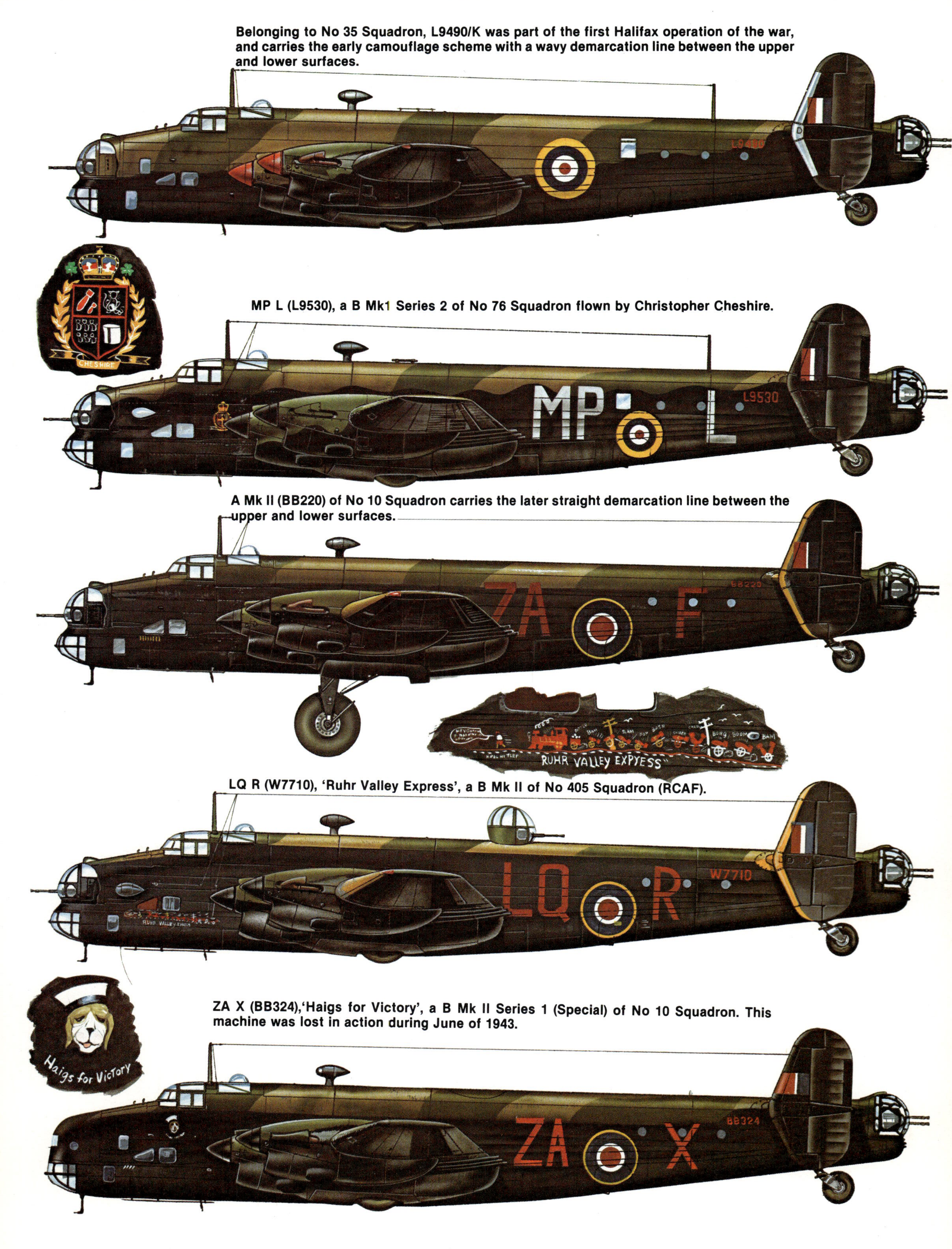

Belonging to No 35 Squadron, L9490/K was part of the first Halifax operation of the war, and carries the early camouflage scheme with a wavy demarcation line between the upper and lower surfaces.

MP L (L9530), a B Mk1 Series 2 of No 76 Squadron flown by Christopher Cheshire.

A Mk II (BB220) of No 10 Squadron carries the later straight demarcation line between the upper and lower surfaces.

LQ R (W7710), 'Ruhr Valley Express', a B Mk II of No 405 Squadron (RCAF).

ZA X (BB324), 'Haigs for Victory', a B Mk II Series 1 (Special) of No 10 Squadron. This machine was lost in action during June of 1943.

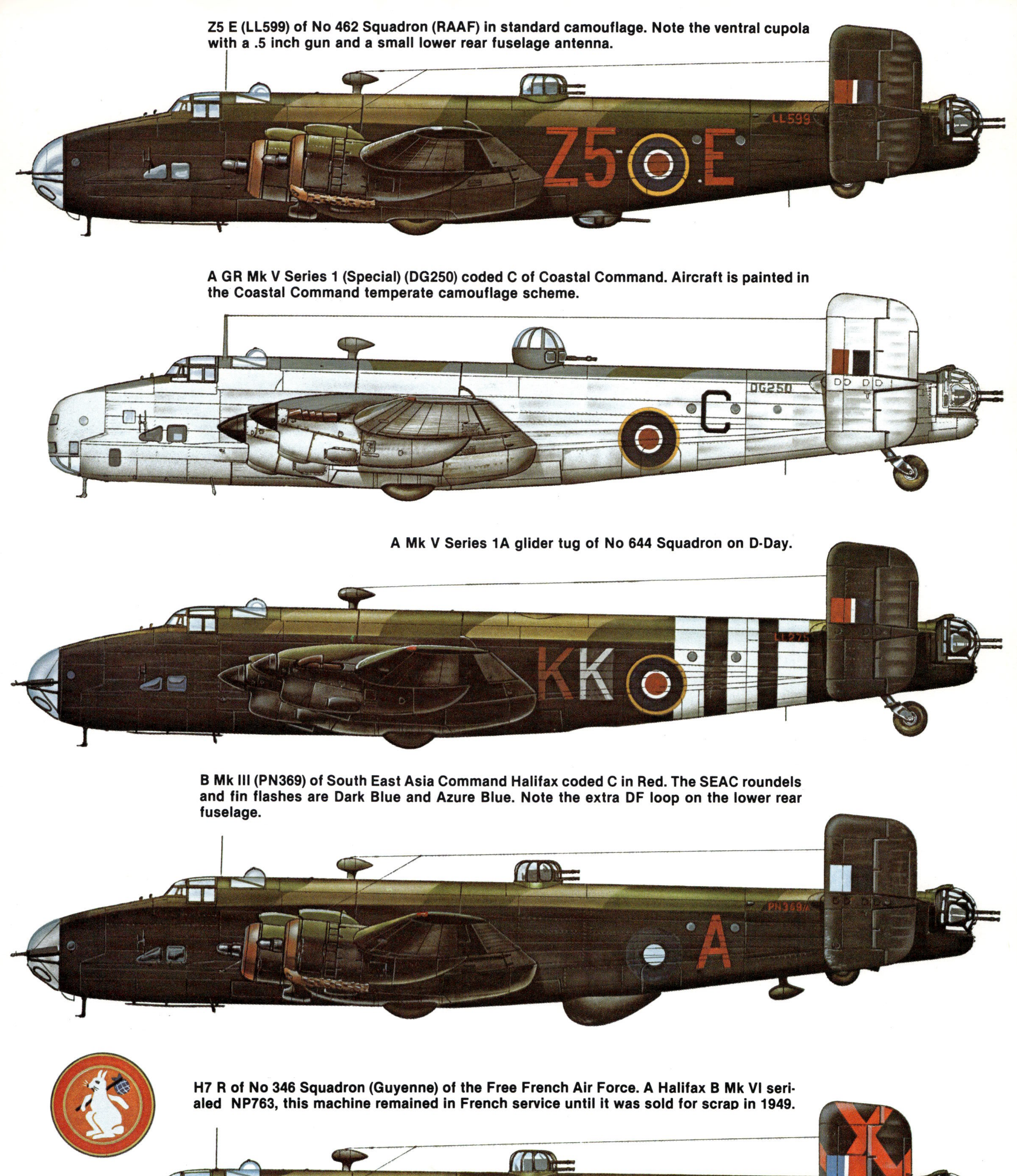

Z5 E (LL599) of No 462 Squadron (RAAF) in standard camouflage. Note the ventral cupola with a .5 inch gun and a small lower rear fuselage antenna.

A GR Mk V Series 1 (Special) (DG250) coded C of Coastal Command. Aircraft is painted in the Coastal Command temperate camouflage scheme.

A Mk V Series 1A glider tug of No 644 Squadron on D-Day.

B Mk III (PN369) of South East Asia Command Halifax coded C in Red. The SEAC roundels and fin flashes are Dark Blue and Azure Blue. Note the extra DF loop on the lower rear fuselage.

H7 R of No 346 Squadron (Guyenne) of the Free French Air Force. A Halifax B Mk VI serialed NP763, this machine remained in French service until it was sold for scrap in 1949.

B MK II Series 1a

During June of 1943, Bomber Command began to receive examples of the Merlin 22 powered Halifax Mk II Series 1a which incorporated the modifications and refinements recommended by A&AEE, and introduced a clear plastic one piece nose cone in place of the so-called 'Z-fairing', increasing overall fuselage length to 71ft, 7in.

The Merlin 22 engines required 100 octane fuel and turned out 1,480 hp at 12,500ft. Rectangular section Morris block radiators replaced the Gallay drum type. This revised radiator air intake shape, without the oil cooler lip, was similar in shape to that of the Halifax I's engines, but with the raked back profile of the Mk II nacelles. Most aircraft also had the lower profile Boulton Paul A Mk VIII turret and a single .303 Vickers K gun positioned to fire from the apex of the new nose cone, which had optically flat panels for bomb aiming.

Relatively few Mk II Series 1a aircraft retained the original vertical tail surfaces for more than a few months since the D-type fin (Mod 814) was quickly introduced on production lines and were retro-fitted to squadron aircraft. A further refinement was some redesign of the bomb doors to fully enclose a 4,000lb bomb. This was achieved by fitting new hinges and side flaps to the original Type A metal doors — which had to be replaced on earlier Marks by faired wooden doors on steel carrier frames to enable them to enclose a 4,000 pounder. Known as Type C, these modified doors were interchangeable with Type D doors fitted to the Halifax III, an arrangement that eliminated the need for bulged doors. The 4,000 pound would be the largest diameter bomb the Halifax was to carry. Two 4,000 pounders joined together made up the maximum single bomb weight of 8,000 lbs.

The prototype Halifax Mk II Series 1a (HR679) flew from Radlett for the first time on 14 December 1942. 299 were built, all by Handley Page.

Further refinement of the Mk II, under the designation Series 1a, introduced the clear nose cone and the flush fitting top turret. This B Mk II Series Ia (HR861) was issued to No 35 Squadron and failed to return from Nuremberg on 18 August 1943. (Aeroplane)

Dispersal at Snaith, Yorkshire, has Halifaxes of No 51 Squadron being readied for the coming night's work. Incendiaries and 500 pounders are being loaded into HR952/X, a B MK II Series 1a lost on a Berlin raid in January 1944. (Aeroplane)

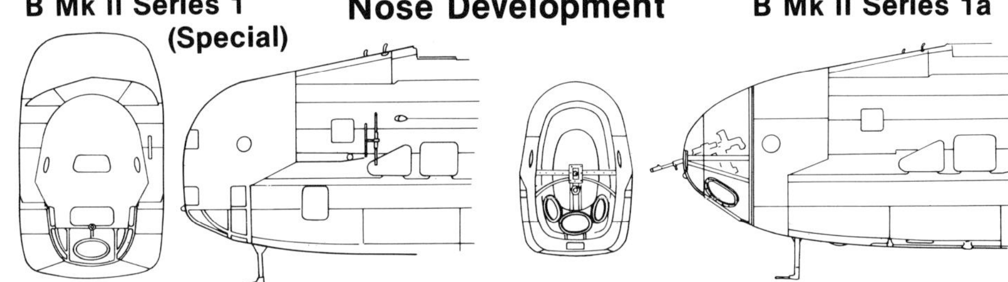

Crowded and water-logged Italian airfield (probably one of the Foggia complex) during the spring of 1944 has a multiplicity of types. The Halifax is almost certainly a No 614 Squadron aircraft, while the P-47s are from the 325th Fighter Group — then without the distinctive checker tails. Other Halifaxes, P-47s and a Wellington can be seen in the background.

B II Series Ia NP-A (JP113) of No 428 Squadron (Ghost) RCAF warming up at Middleton St. George, County Durham, on 4 April 1944. Attacked by a night fighter while on a sortie to Lens on 21 April, the aircraft made a crash landing at Attlebridge, Norfolk. 'Git Up Them Stairs' has the red maple leaf of Canada and a red Pegasus over the mission scoreboard of seventeen bombing raids and seven supply drops. Installation of the 1,480 hp Merlin 22 engines and replacement of the Gallay drum type radiator with the Morris block radiators caused a redesign of the airscoop. (RCAF)

B Mk II Series 1 (Special)

Merlin XX Engines with Gallay Radiators

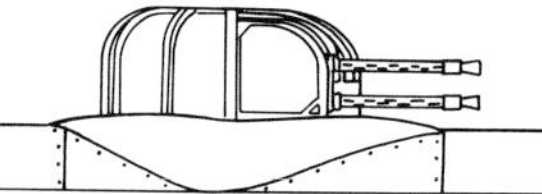

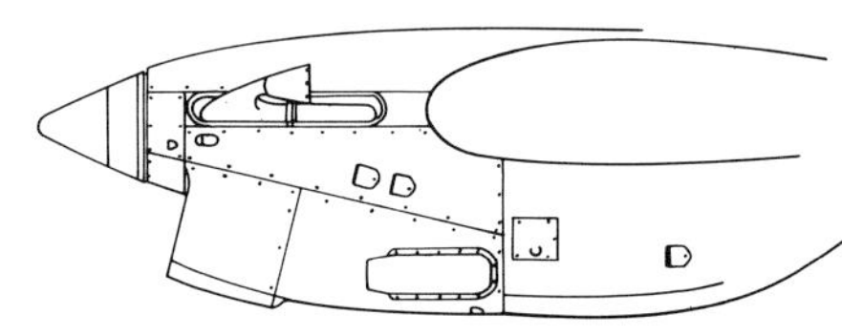

Raised Turret

B Mk II Series 1a

Merlin 22 Engines with Morris Block Radiators

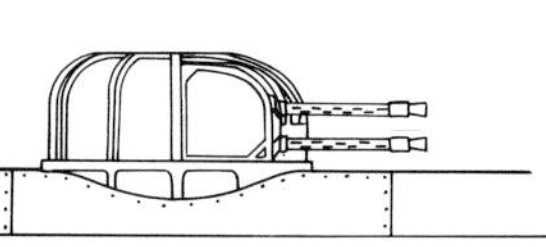

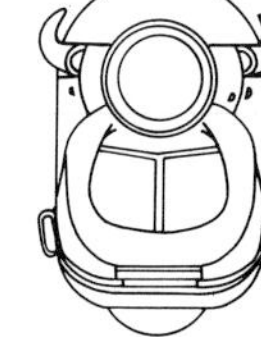

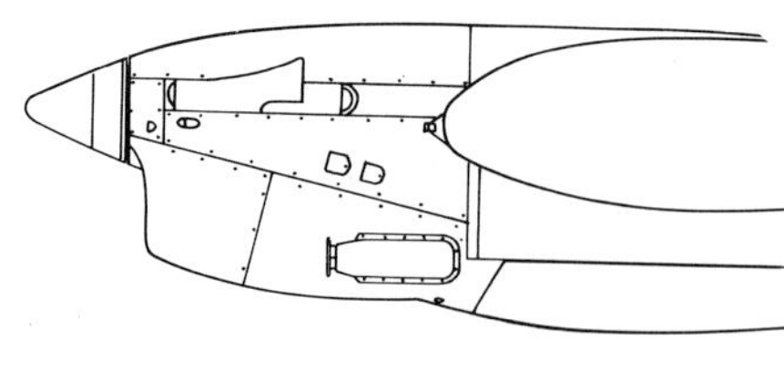

Flush Turret

No 35 Squadron was one of the five premier units of the Path Finder Force when it formed in August of 1942. One of its outstanding bombing leaders was Alec Cranswick, whose Halifax B II Series Ia is seen here. Coded TL L (HR926) had its starboard side serial directly over the code letter, giving the appearance of a Z. The aircraft was lost over Kassel in October 1943, and Cranswick himself was later shot down in a Lancaster in July 1944. (R. L. Ward)

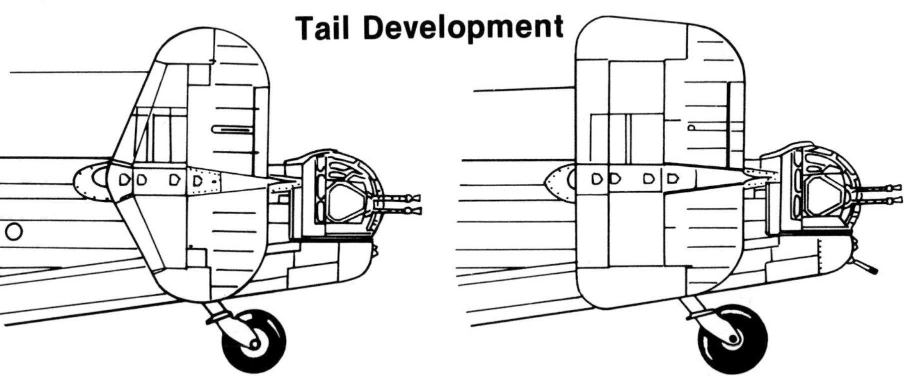

Tail Development

Mk II Series 1a (Early)　　　　**Mk II Series 1a (Late)**

Halifax B II Series Ia of No 78 Squadron on an air test from its base at Breighton, Yorks, during the autumn of 1943. Modification 814, providing enlarged vertical tail surfaces, was quickly introduced on the assembly line and operational aircraft were retrofitted with the new tail surfaces as quickly as possible.

B MK V SERIES 1 (SPECIAL) (HP 63)

Because of a shortage of the British Messier undercarriage it was decided to fit the Dowty levered suspension type of undercarriage to the Halifax. This type of landing gear had proven very reliable on both the Manchester and the Lancaster. Since the designation B Mk III had been reserved for the Hercules radial powered Halifax already well into development and the designation B Mk IV was reserved for the Rolls-Royce 65 powered HP 60A project (eventually abandoned), the Dowty suspension equipped Halifax was designated B Mk V. Produced in parallel with the B Mk II with which, except for the landing gear, it was identical, the B Mk V was delivered to operational units in June of 1943.

After tests to find compatible lubricants and seals, Dowty commenced production for the Halifax, whereupon an inherent weakness was revealed in the castings used. Since little could be done to remedy the situation, if Halifax output was not to be seriously disrupted, Mk V production continued with landing weight being restricted to 40,000 lbs.

For this reason the majority of Mk Vs were allocated to meteorological reconnaissance and maritime patrol duties, glider tug and transport work, although No. 6 Group (RCAF) squadrons and Nos. 76, 346 and 347 Squadrons of Bomber Command operated them for a limited period. Mk Vs were totally withdrawn from operations against German targets in February of 1944.

Leeming scene on 16 November 1943, shows groundcrewmen 'gremlin hunting' at A Apple's dispersal. One of the no 427 (Lion) Squadron's B Mk Vs EB241 had sortied twenty-one times by this date. More trips were undoubtedly added before the aircraft passed to 1664 HCU for less hazardous duty until 1 November 1945, when it was struck off charge. (RCAF)

Supporting Bomber Command's front-line squadrons were the Heavy Conversion Units (HCU). One of 17 Halifax HCUs was 1664, which was based at Croft, Yorks, when this B V Series I (Special) serialed EB199 was lost in a crash in October of 1943. (R. L. Ward)

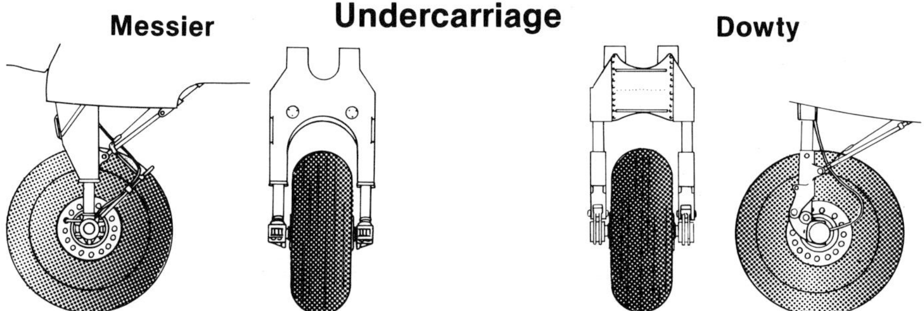

No 434 'Bluenose' Squadron RCAF was formed on Halifax Vs in June of 1943. This aircraft (LK953) served with No 428 and No 427 Squadrons as well as No 434 at different periods. It was lost in November of 1943. (R. L. Ward)

Canada's exposure to American cartoon characters was reflected in RCAF bomber nose art. Old favorite Popeye adorned WL P (LL288) of No 434 Squadron, having 'spinached' the enemy eight times by 16 November 1943. Passing to 1659 HCU P Popeye swung on take off from Topcliffe the following May and ripped off its landing gear. (RCAF)

B Mk V Series 1a

The Halifax Mk V Series 1a was identical to the Mk II Series 1a apart from the Dowty landing gear. Late production aircraft had Merlin 22s with ejector exhausts and four bladed Rotol propellers, although a handful of aircraft flew operations with four bladed airscrews on the outboard engines and three-bladed ones inboard. B Mk V production terminated in January of 1944, after 904 aircraft had been delivered by Fairey Aviation and Rootes Securities.

Another Bluenose MK V was EB217/A, 'Alie-Oop'. The two color spinners (believed to be Yellow and Black) were carried by a number of the squadron's Halifax Vs. (R.L. Ward)

Halifax B Mk III (HP 61)

The mating of Bristol Hercules radial engines to the refined airframe incorporating all the improvements of the later Merlin-engined aircraft finally turned the Halifax into a good, reliable airplane. Bristol Hercules VI engines had first been test flown in a B Mk II (R9534) which would serve as the Mk III prototype, at Boscombe Down in March of 1943. Later that year D-type fins were fitted and other modifications were made to this and the first production aircraft (HX227), which made its maiden flight on 29 August. B Mk III production aircraft were powered by Hercules XVI engines which more than made up for the performance deficiencies of earlier Halifaxes. The tailwheel was made to retract fully, although the bottom of the tire projected into the slipstream when lying flat, there being no tail wheel doors.

No 466 Squadron (RAAF) was the first to receive Halifax Mk IIIs in November of 1943, and thereafter issue of the new Bristol powered aircraft to Bomber Command was rapid. Aircraft were initially not fitted with H2S but working parties had four squadrons fully equipped with radar by the end of the year. On 1 December No 466 flew its first Mk III sorties, laying mines off Terschelling.

Most Halifax squadrons maintained a mix of Mk IIs and Vs while transitioning to radial engined Mk IIIs, but by mid-January of 1944, nine squadrons had received examples. In February of 1944, after nearly eighteen months of testing with various types, a ventral gun position was finally certified for operational service. This was the Preston-Green mounting with a single .5in Browning in a dome shaped cupola with five transparent windows. It could only be fitted in place of the H2S cupola and was in approximately the same location. However squadrons occasionally made their own modifications to the installation by doubling the number of guns and removing the seat provided to give a better field of fire. It was also not unusual for the cupola windows to be faired in or painted over to reduce glare.

All five contractual groups contributed to Halifax III production, which ran to 2,127 aircraft, more than any other variant. Early B Mk IIIs had the 98ft, 10in, wingspan of the Rolls-Royce engined Marks, although the majority of Mk IIIs were built or retro-fitted with extended wingtips, bringing the span to 104ft, 2in.

Maximum weight of the Mk III was 65,000lbs, including a 13,000lb bomb load and a total

fuel capacity of 1,986 gallons, including two 90 gallon tanks in each outer wing bomb cell. Each wing still contained six fuel tanks, although the No 2 tanks were moved to the leading edge of the center section from their previous location between the engine nacelles. Overload tanks could be fitted in the bomb bay providing an absolute maximum fuel load of 2,688 gallons. Range of the Halifax III was 1,770 miles, and service ceiling was 20,000 ft. Maximum speed at 6,000 feet was 277 mph with a 225 mph economical cruising speed of 20,000 feet.

Mid-1944 saw the introduction of additional new devices to provide the bomber force some measure of protection in an increasingly hostile environment; these included Fishpond, a revised version of the Monica tail warning system with a visual rather than aural indication.

Path Finder Force had relinquished all of its Halifaxes by March of 1944. Only No 35

A textbook landing for one of No 432 (Leaside) Squadron's B Mk IIIs at East Moor, Yorkshire, on 28 November 1944. The Hercules XVI radial engine enclosed in Beaufighter type cowlings turned the Halifax into a good reliable bomber that was capable of penetrating deep into Reich territory. (RCAF)

R9534 was one of the test-bed Halifaxes that was used to prove various installations for service use. Early in 1943 it became the prototype Mk III, fitted with Bristol Hercules VI radial engines.

The Halifax tail turret remained much the same throughout its service life. Apart from a small number of new turrets introduced toward the end of the war, tail defense was provided by the Boulton Paul Type E turret, seen here with the gun breech covers open. (IWM)

The gas-operated Vickers K nose gun mounted in the late production Merlin-engined marks and the majority of Hercules-powered Halifaxes was not regarded as an effective weapon; however, it did occasionally give a good account of itself. (M. Wright)

Flight Sergeant Jack 'Junior' Cumbers in the Boulton Paul Type A mid upper turret of a Halifax B III of No 424 (Tiger) Squadron RCAF. The compact turret greatly improved the Halifax's chance of survival when attacked by night fighters. (RCAF)

Cowling Development

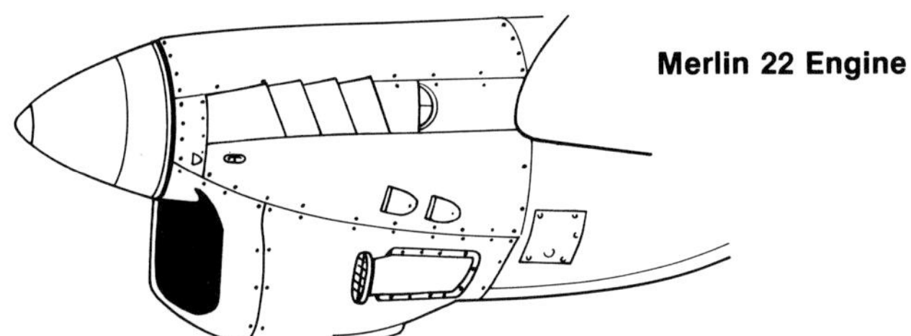

B Mk II Series 1a

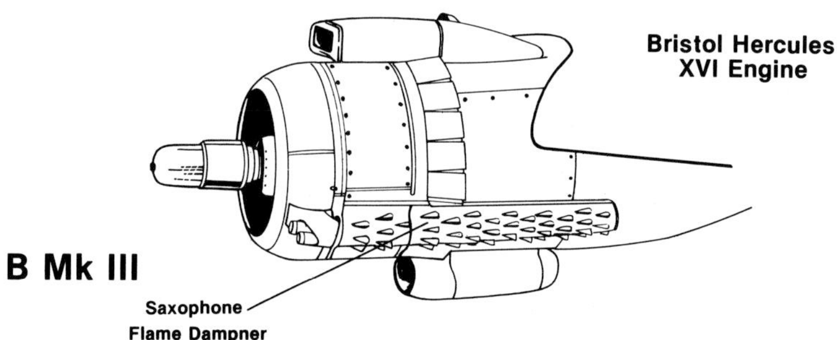

B Mk III

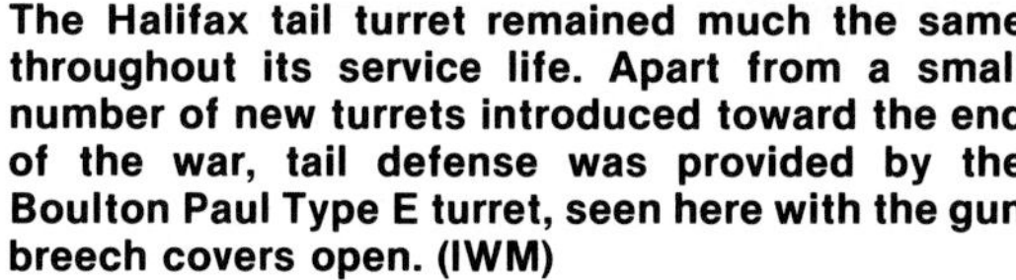

No 77 Squadron B III KN G (MZ359) formates with another Halifax over the English countryside in the vicinity of its base at Full Sutton, Yorkshire. This particular Halifax survived the war. Initial production Mk IIIs did not carry H2S; however, as sets became available, they were installed on the production line and work teams went into the field to retrofit them to service aircraft.

Squadron had retained its Mk IIIs throughout the notorious Battle of Berlin, the series of raids on the German capital and other targets which cost Bomber Command well over 1,000 aircraft. This grim campaign started on the night of 15/16 November 1943, and lasted through the end of March 1944. There were sixteen attacks carried out on Berlin and nineteen on cities such as Stuttgart, Brunswick, Stettin, Schweinfurt and Essen. Then, on 30/31 March came the raid on Nuremburg, which alone cost Bomber Command over one hundred aircraft.

During the weeks preceding D-Day, Bomber Command undertook a series of raids on communications targets in France, German radar stations and fortifications along the 'West Wall'. Although the results were mixed, RAF heavies were often called upon to hit very small targets with the minimum possible casualties among the French civilian population — in effect carrying out daylight precision bombing which was the USAAF's forte and Bomber Command's original method of attack. On the eve of the invasion, the RAF had 22 first line Halifax squadrons split equally between No 4 and 6 Groups.

Shortly before the end, No 100 Group, the RAF's bomber support group, began to standardize on Halifaxes as its main type. Large enough to accommodate the bulky electronic devices vital to No 100's role, the Halifax was used operationally by four squadrons and two special duties flights, B IIIs being the most common variant. Equipped with Mandrel and Airborne Cigar jammers, as well as vast quantities of Window, these machines flew a variety of jamming and bombing sorties to materially protect Main Force squadrons.

Jamming was also the intended role of the B IIIs of No 1341 Flight operating from Digri, India, from May, 1945. Equipped with a second D/F loop fairing below the rear fuselage, these aircraft found little 'trade' in sorties against primitive Japanese radars, but carried out a useful pathfinding role for bombing strikes by long range Liberators.

No 462 (RAAF) Squadron Halifax B III with full 'Airborne Cigar' fit for radar-jamming duties. Of additional interest are the wing-tip 'Pipe Rack' jammer whip aerials, the 'Window' chutes forward of the bomb doors and aft of the H2S cupola and the bulged fairings on the inner sections of the bomb doors. 'Jane' also carries No 4 Group daylight identification markings of three yellow vertical tail stripes, even though it was part of No 100 (BS) Group from January of 1945. (M. Wright)

One of Tholthorpe's dispersal areas in July 1944, has PT B (MZ420) a B MK III 'The Bird of Prey' and an unidentified sister Halifax being readied for the night's grim work ahead. (RCAF)

The ventral defense problem was not so easily solved, although there was a fair number of Preston Green cupolas fitted to Halifaxes. Mounting one, occasionally two, machine guns, it was comforting for crews to know that the belly of their aircrfaft was not completely unprotected. This B III KW M (MZ954) of No 425 (Alouette) Squadron RCAF, carried one ventral gun at Tholthorpe, Yorks, on 29 November 1943. As its name implies, the unit was composed of mostly French Canadians. (RCAF)

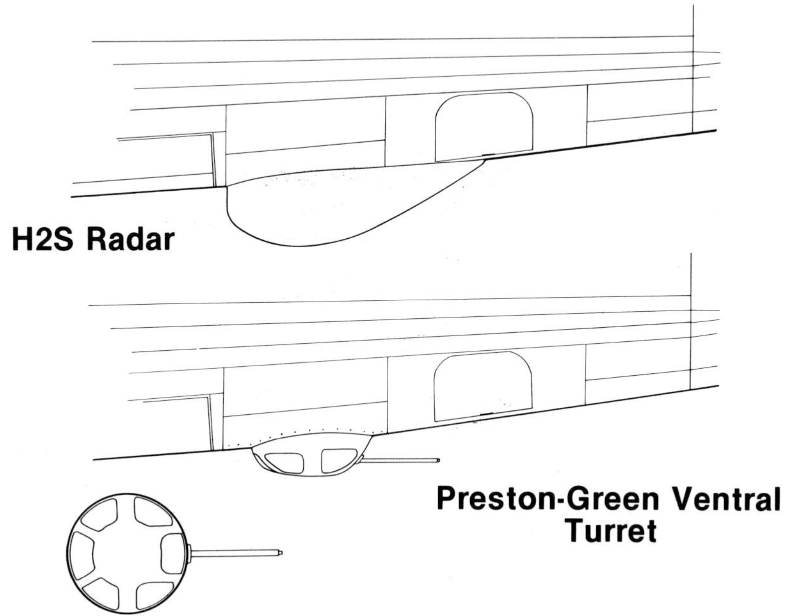

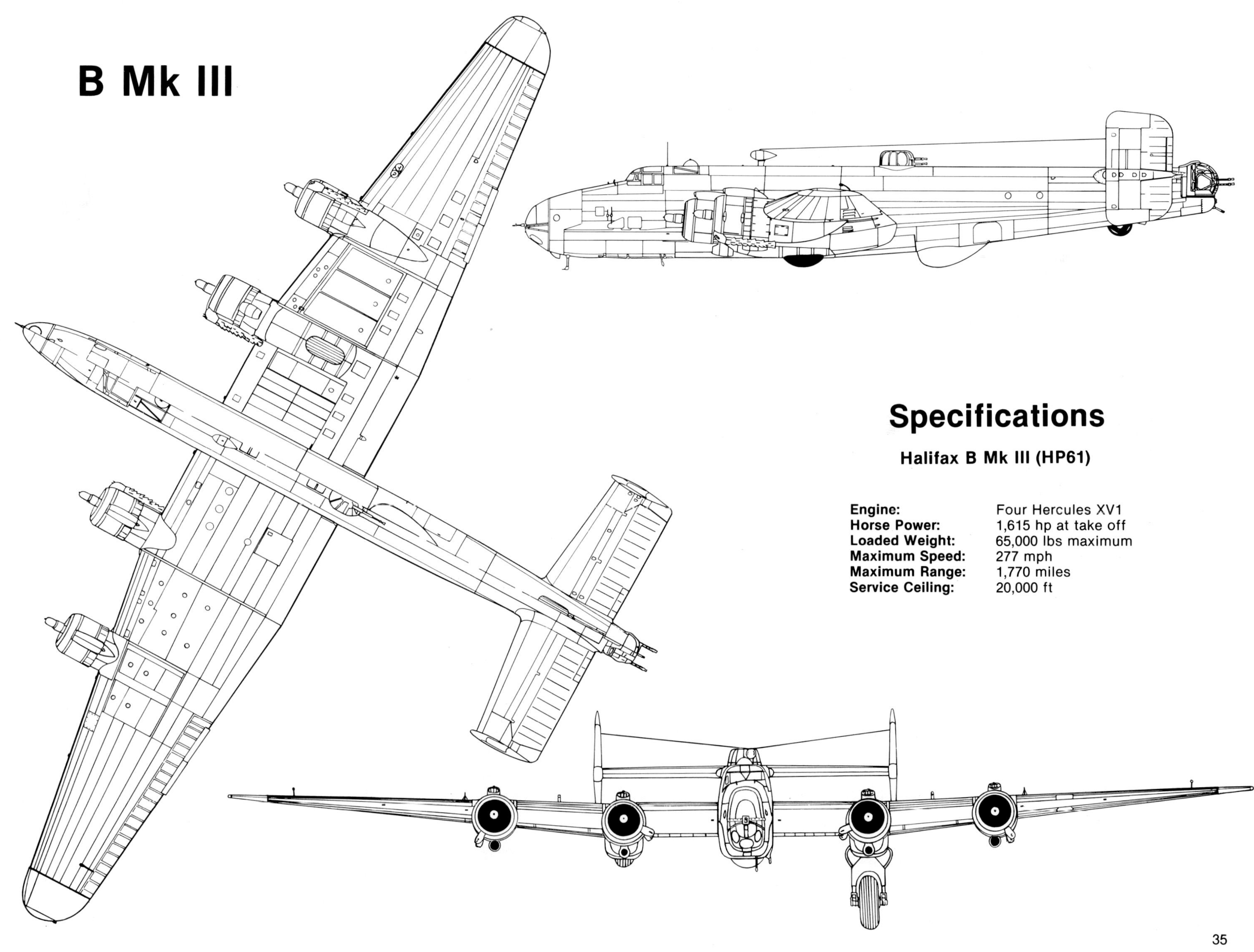

B Mk III

Specifications

Halifax B Mk III (HP61)

Engine: Four Hercules XV1
Horse Power: 1,615 hp at take off
Loaded Weight: 65,000 lbs maximum
Maximum Speed: 277 mph
Maximum Range: 1,770 miles
Service Ceiling: 20,000 ft

This Halifax B Mk III (LV833), which was issued to No 466 (RAAF) Squadron, displays its upper surface camouflage pattern. The aircraft was lost on operations in July of 1944. LV833 has not been retro-fitted with the extended wing tips. (Aeroplane)

Wing Development

B Mk II
98 ft. 10 in.

B Mk III
104 ft. 2 in.

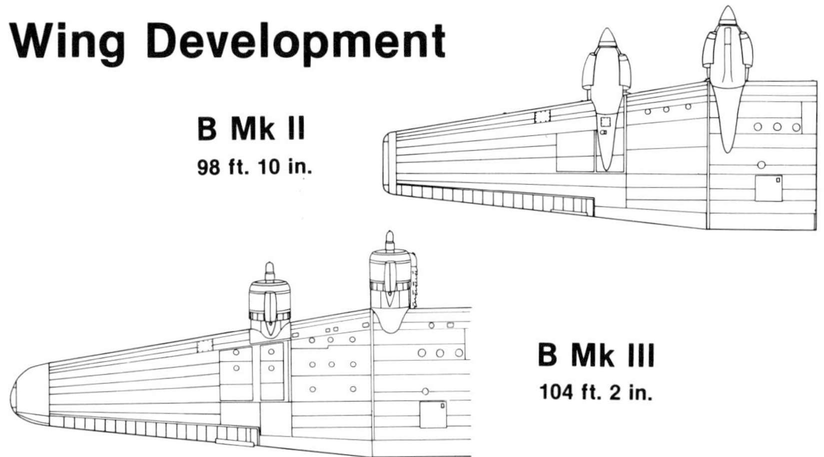

No 462 Squadron also had Halifax IIIs equipped with 'Mandrel' jammers, most of the aerials for which are shown in this view. This aircraft has bulged attachments on the bomb doors, the purpose of which is obscure. Here, they appear to be lights of some kind, whereas these that are on Z5 N 'Jane', seen on page 34, seem to be solid fairings. (M. Wright)

Halifax B Mk III of No 192 (Special Duties) Squadron configured for a dual bombing and electronic intelligence gathering role. Operating a variety of aircraft, No 192 only employed Halifaxes for this double task from January of 1945. Part of the ECM task was to drop 'Window' as a contribution to the Special Window Force of No 100 Group. (M. Wright)

A 1341 Flight B Mk III used for ELINT sorties against Japanese radars just before the end of the war. As well as SEAC markings, these aircraft carried an extra DF loop forward of the tailwheel. (R. L. Ward)

Interesting nose art on a 1341 Flight B Mk III at Digri, India, in 1945. (IWM)

SEAC Halifax of 1341 Flight (PN369/A) carrying the revised markings and ventral DF loop which can be seen just forward of the tail wheel. (IWM)

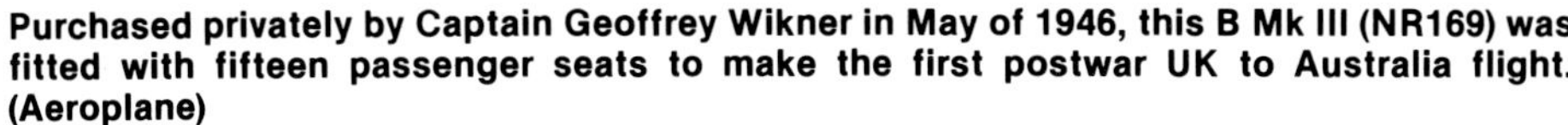

Captain Wikner's Halifax at Radlett after civilian conversion on 16 April. Apart from the British civil registration, most wartime markings of No 466 Squadron (RAAF), including the yellow tail stripes, were retained for the flight, which was completed on 29 April 1946. (Aeroplane)

Purchased privately by Captain Geoffrey Wikner in May of 1946, this B Mk III (NR169) was fitted with fifteen passenger seats to make the first postwar UK to Australia flight. (Aeroplane)

Empire Air Navigation School B Mk III (PN441) 'Keehal' during a liaison flight to Burma and India in January of 1946. This photo was taken at Barrackpur. (Robertson)

Halifax B Mk VII (HP 61)

Entering squadron service out of numerical sequence, the Halifax B Mk VII was an interim version developed to offset slow production of the improved Hercules 100 engine, intended for the B Mk VI. Consequently the B Mk VII was powered by Hercules XVIs but incorporated a redesigned fuel system intended for the new Hercules 100 engine. Seven flexible main tanks in each wing provided a fuel capacity of 2,196 gallons, each No 2 tank being located in the outer wing bomb cells.

Extended wing tips were standard on the B Mk VII, as was the H2S cupola, factory installed ventral gun turrets being dispensed with. Larger Gallay oil coolers and a revised cabin heating system also distinguished the Mk VII, although these changes were not externally evident apart from the addition of a small rear fuselage air scoop for the rear turret heater, first introduced on late production B Mk IIIs.

Operational use of the Mk VII as a bomber was restricted to three No 6 Group squadrons, the first being No 426 at Linton-on-Ouse in mid-June 1944.

C 'Chesty' (NP780), a B MkVII of No 408 Squadron, survived into the postwar era to be sold for scrap in December of 1949 (R.L. Ward)

Impressive scoreboard on EQ P (NP754), a B Mk VII of No 408 (Goose) Squadron RCAF at Linton-on-Ouse. (R. L. Ward

Halifax B Mk VI

When Hercules 100 engines became available in quantity from February of 1944, the Halifax was to reach a performance peak in the B Mk VI. With the revised fuel system using 100-octane fuel, this upgraded powerplant provided 1,675 hp for take-off, giving the aircraft a top speed of 312 mph and a range of 2,350 miles. Ceiling was raised to 24,000ft at a maximum weight of 68,000lbs. Bomb load remained the same as that for earlier variants at 13,000lbs.

In the event, only three squadrons, the Free French Nos 346 and 347, and No 158 RAF, were equipped with Mk VIs before the end of hostilities in Europe and these participated in the final assault on the Third Reich during the spring of 1945. By then Bomber Command was regularly flying daylight sorties and individual aircraft reported skirmishes with German jet fighters. To better defend themselves against this new foe some Halifaxes were fitted with a Boulton Paul Type D rear turret armed with two .5in machine guns. To direct his fire the gunner had radar, code named 'Village Inn' in a fairing below the turret housing the receiver. Not fully developed before the war ended, this Airborne Gun Laying Turret (AGLT) was fitted to only a small number of Halifaxes.

Pakistan was the final operator of the Mk VI when the air force bought seven in 1948.

When the two Free French Halifax squadrons in Bomber Command, No 346 (Guyenne) and No 347 (Tunisie), had finished their war service flying from Elvington, Yorkshire, they both went home, taking their Halifax B Mk VIs with them. Home was initially Bordeaux/Merignac, a base previously used by the Heinkel He 177s of Kampfgeschwader 40. Ten Halifaxes can be seen in residence. (ECPA)

With the end of the war in Europe, many Halifaxes rested briefly at Maintenance Units before being broken up. This B VI (RG610) of No 102 Squadron, retained the unit's 4 Group daylight identification markings of two horizontal red tail bands as well as its serial in white under the wings while at No 29 Maintenance Unit (MU) at High Ercall in February of 1946. (IWM)

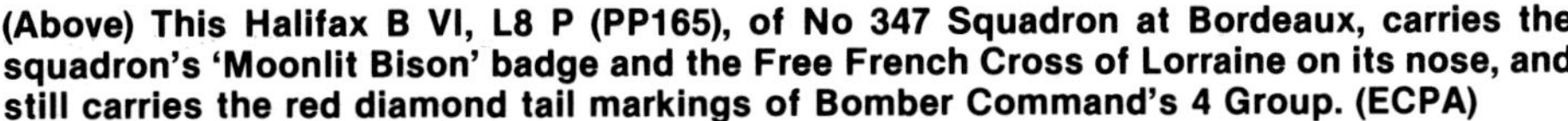

(Above) This Halifax B VI, L8 P (PP165), of No 347 Squadron at Bordeaux, carries the squadron's 'Moonlit Bison' badge and the Free French Cross of Lorraine on its nose, and still carries the red diamond tail markings of Bomber Command's 4 Group. (ECPA)

(Above Right) H7 D a Halifax B Mk VI (believed to be RG609) of No 346 (Guyenne) Squadron during the early postwar period. Halifax H7 G (RG491) can be seen on the right. (ECPA)

(Right) As well as aircraft maintenance, the French needed to make repairs to their battered airfield. In the meantime, Halifax pre-flight checks were carried out with available equipment. The nearest is H7 H (PG562) of No 346 Squadron. (ECPA)

(Below Right) Gradually postwar markings were applied to the Halifaxes in French service. Large prewar roundel dimensions replaced the reverse shades of RAF 'C' type fuselage roundels, and rudder striping was again applied. The nearest of these two B Mk VIs retains its H2S cupola along with the addition of a freight pannier — an unusual combination on any Halifax. (ECPA)

(Below) Integrated into the postwar Armee de l'Air, the Halifax squadrons took French designations, as Groupes de Bombardement GB II/23 'Guyenne' (No 346 Squadron) and GB I/25 'Tunisie' (No 346 Squadron). This eighty-one mission B Mk III carries the combined rabbit and bird device of the Guyenne unit painted in Arabic numerals as '2/23' and is fitted with a belly freight pannier. (ECPA)

GENERAL RECONNAISSANCE VARIANTS

The specialized needs of Coastal Command led to a number of detail changes to the Halifax bomber variants used for long range patrol duties from the winter of 1942/43, prior to which No 158 and 405 Squadrons of Bomber Command had been temporarily detached for Coastal duties between October 1942 and March 1943. On 18 October 1942, twenty Halifax B Mk IIs were transferred to Coastal Command principally to perform anti-U-boat patrols into the Bay of Biscay. These aircraft were the initial equipment of No 58 and 502 (Ulster) Squadrons when they achieved full conversion to Halifaxes by February, 1943.

GR MK II Series 1 (SPECIAL)

Halifaxes converted to the GR role were from Rootes production, being reworked by Cunliffe-Owen at Eastleigh, Hampshire. Apart from their predominantly white Coastal Command finish (stipulated from 1 February, 1943) these machines were externally similar to Bomber Command B MK II Specials, with Merlin XX engines and the Z fairing or glazed nose in place of the nose turret. Most known examples had the low profile A Mk VIII dorsal turret, either with or without the raised decking, although there is some evidence to suggest that certain Coastal aircraft retained the Hudson type dorsal turret for a time. Contemporary reports also mention beam guns being used, indicating a degree of squadron level modification to increase armament rather than reduce it, as Bomber Command Halifaxes had been forced to do.

Installation of ASV Mk III (H2S equivalent) radar was an urgent priority and by May, 1943, most operational aircraft were so equipped; Boozer IFF equipment was also a standard fitting.

Initially using Mark VII naval depth charges adapted for aircraft use, the two GR Halifax squadrons soon received 600lb depth bombs filled with Torpex explosive which greatly increased the chances of fatal damage to U-boats. Up to six could be accommodated on the wing racks of the Halifax.

The ability to carry its offensive load in the wings enabled the Halifax to be a useful anti-U-boat weapon and at the same time operate at extreme ranges carrying extra fuel tanks in the fuselage bomb bay. Tests by the Coastal Command Development Unit (CCDU) showed that the maximum endurance of the Halifax could be as much as sixteen hours, although a limit of twelve to thirteen hours was made to provide a margin of safety.

The CCDU tested a variety of aids and weapons for Coastal aircraft in general, one being installation of a Leigh Light under the forward fuselage of the Halifax. There are, however, no records of the Halifax using the light operationally, U-boat attacks being made either by radar detection or by the 'moonpath' method at night. Widespread use was also made of high illumination flares.

With full armament and fuel, some Coastal Halifaxes operated above the maximum weight limit at over 61,000lbs with little adverse effect, and later Halifax GR Mk Vs were cleared for an all-up weight of 65,000lbs.

This GR II Series 1 (Special) (JD376) became a test aircraft after initially being issued to No 78 Squadron and 1663 Heavy Conversion Unit. It eventually passed to the Royal Aircraft Establishment and was photographed at Boscombe Down in April of 1945. The interim type of dorsal turret fairing has been fitted in this view.

Part of a batch of 250 GR Mk IIs built by Handley Page, HR744/G served with No 58 Squadron until being struck off charge in November of 1944. Its Coastal Command fittings include the extra nose bracing for the .5 Browning and ASV Mk III radar in the cupola. The individual fuselage coding 'O' is grouped with a small figure '1', and is believed to be an interim style of presentation by the squadron, which adopted the code 'BY' during the last months of the war. (M. Wright)

GR Mk II
Series 1A

An important change made specifically for Coastal work in this variant was the installation of a .5in Browning machine gun in the extreme nose. Replacing the Vickers K in all Coastal Halifaxes, the single 'fifty' being extremely useful for clearing a surfaced U-boat's AA gun crew during target run-in. Belt fed, it required additional bracing with metal struts to secure it in the transparent nose cone.

The first GR Mk II Series Ia was JP258 with Merlin XX engines and Gallay radiators, and four-blade Rotol airscrews, a by no means unusual combination on GR Mk IIs. Engine exhausts were both standard and of final Merlin type consisting of four pipe ejectors and a flame damper.

(Right) Passing to its sister squadron, No 58, JP328 had an appropriate change of codes. Photographed in a Halifax 'graveyard', it was struck off charge in May of 1945. (IWM)

The other GR squadron equipped with Halifaxes in Coastal Command was No 502. This GR Mk II Series Ia (JP328) has the late-war anti-shipping finish, which is very similar to the scheme used on Bomber Command Halifaxes. A point of interest is the white starboard side spinners, while the port side spinners are black. (H. Holmes)

Halifax GR Mk V
Series 1A

The most standardized and widely used Coastal Halifaxs, the GR Mk V had Merlin 22s using 100 octane fuel, Morris block radiators, and four bladed propellers. Early or late pattern exhausts were used, but all had Dowty landing gear.

Late war anti-shipping strikes by Coastal Command saw Halifaxes using medium capacity bombs of 250 and 500lb weight. Mk XIV bomb sights had also replaced the older Mk VII by the time the anti-shipping phase began in June of 1944. Not that attacks on U-boats had ceased — indeed, the last of nine U-boats sunk by Halifaxes was not despatched until 17 October 1944. And at the end of the conflict, Coastal Halifaxes of the two GR squadrons had sunk over 26,000 tons of shipping. Since a considerable number of such strikes were at night, Coastal Halifaxes were repainted in a more appropriate 'night' finish.

Halifax Met Mk V

Operating under Coastal Command during the war were three meteorological (Met) squadrons equipped with Halifaxes — No 517, 518 and 520 Squadrons. Tasked with the vital duty of gathering weather data, these aircraft carried a Met officer and instrumentation to take temperature readings, measure sea level pressure and record wind velocity.

Gee or Loran equipment enabled navigators to fly very precise tracks at predetermined altitudes and ranges on two main types of flight patterns under the code names 'Mercer' and 'Bismuth'. The information obtained was radioed home at set intervals, collated and relayed by teleprinter for use by all RAF commands.

Halifax GR Mk IIIA/ Mk III

Use of the Hercules powered Halifax in Coastal Command during WWII was limited, No 502 Squadron receiving its first Mk IIIA in December, 1944. The A suffix referred to Coastal Command equipment, while the Mk IIIs were virtually standard aircraft. No 58 Squadron did not receive its first Mk IIIs until April of 1945, and those sorties flown (by both squadrons), are believed to have been exclusively against shipping, necessitating the night finish.

Halifax Met Mk III

No 517 Squadron was the first met Halifax unit to get Mk IIIs, in February of 1945. No 518 followed suit in March and No 520 recorded delivery of its first Mk IIIA in April. There was little time to make extensive use of the new variant before the end of hostilities, although these three units continued to use Halifaxes in the postwar period, and were joined by No 519 and 521 Squadrons in August and December of 1945, respectively.

Halifax Met Mk VI

No 518 and 521 Squadrons used the Met Mk VI until 1946, when most Halifaxes were withdrawn and the Met squadrons disbanded. The sole exception was No 518 Squadron, being renumbered No 202 Squadron on 1 October 1946. As such it retained its Mk VIs until 1952, when the squadron had the distinction of flying the last Halifax sortie in the RAF on 17 March 1952.

Just before Halifax Met VIs of No 224 Squadron were due to fly home from Gibralter to St. Athan, Cornwall, for scrapping in 1952, a Polish pilot made a heavy landing in B B (RG839). The partial Coastal Command white finish was adopted for some of the last Halifaxes operational in the RAF. (R. L. Ward)

AIRBORNE FORCES VARIANTS

The Airborne Forces Development Unit began trials with the Halifax B II in October of 1941, aiming to meet a dual requirement for a paratroop transport, and a glider tug for the Airspeed Horsa and Waco Hadrian. Later the Halifax became the only aircraft capable of towing the 110ft span General Aircraft Hamilcar loaded to 7.8 tons and able to haul a light tank. These Airborne Forces Halifaxes were designated A Mk II.

Early A Mk II conversions had rudimentary paratroop seating and a circular ventral dropping hatch. A winch was fitted to gather parachute static lines, and to reduce some of the slipstream while a jump was being made. A semicircular windshield was fitted over the jump opening.

The first operation involving Halifax glider tugs with Horsas was the disastrous mission on the night of 19/20 November 1941. In a desperate attempt to land sabotage parties at the Norwegian heavy water plant, suspected of being used by the Germans for atomic research, two Halifax tug-Horsa glider combinations were used. Only one Halifax returned, both gliders and all their occupants being lost.

Halifax A Mk V Series 1 (SPECIAL)

The Mk V became the main Airborne Forces variantsually dispensing with the single forward gun, these aircraft differed little from GR machines, although they did not generally carry H2S. The majority of met flights were made by Mk Vs.

Halifax Mk V, believed to be from No 295 Squadron, towing an Airspeed Horsa glider during the invasion period.

Halifax A Mk V Series 1A

By D-Day both No 38 Group Halifax squadrons had re-equipped with the improved Mk V Series 1A with Merlin 22s and Morris block radiators. The necessary attachments and fittings for paradrops were retained, as was the glider hook. In common with other Airborne Forces Halifaxes, dorsal turrets were not fitted.

Halifax A Mk III

Otherwise similar to their bomber counterparts, 30 A Mk III conversions had Airborne Forces modifications and lacked dorsal turrets. Both No 38 Group squadrons used A Mk IIIs to tow Horsas and Hamilcars into the Arnhem drop zones, although A Mk Vs were issued to the two Albemarle squadrons, Nos 296 and 297 at that time. Both units were to retain the earlier mark until early 1945.

Both A Mk IIIs and A Mk Vs undertook OPERATION VARSITY, the final glider assault of the European war, four Halifaxes being lost out of a total strength of 120. The final weeks of the war saw Airborne Forces Halifaxes engaged on a diversity of tasks including some tactical bombing, SOE work, supply dropping and the ferrying of occupation troops to Norway. All A Mk IIIs were built by Rootes.

No 644 Squadron Halifax A Mk IIIAs preparing for a supply drop. The nearest aircraft is believed to be NA127. (IWM)

Halifax A Mk III (NA425) of No 190 (GT) Squadron carrying a windshield in front of the paratroop dropping hatch and the glider hook under the rear fuselage.

A Mk VII

The Rhine crossing operation saw No 298 Squadron operating seven examples of the penultimate Airborne Forces Halifax, the A Mk VII. Externally similar to the A Mk III in basic form, the A Mk VII was the first to be fitted with a freight pannier of 8,000lb capacity projecting below the bomb bay in place of the bomb doors. A trial installation with the pannier had been made in February of 1945, with LV838, a Mk III as the test bed, and aircraft so equipped were operational before hostilities ceased.

Equipping with Halifaxes in the closing months of the war, No 620 Squadron was based at Aqir, Palestine, when exercise 'Kick-Off III' took place on 2 February 1946. One of the squadron's A Mk VIIs (NA376) is seen dropping a stick of paratroopers over the Yibna Drop Zone. (D. Taylor)

According to records, the Royal Aircraft Establishment operated this A Mk VII (PP350) from delivery in the fall of 1945 to the spring of 1952. The freight pannier has been removed in this view.

A Mk IX (HP 71)

The last Halifax variant built, the A Mk IX was specifically for Airborne Forces use. The port side entrance door was deleted in favor of a rectangular paratroop hatch in the floor, which was strengthened to accommodate sixteen troops seated on each side of the fuselage aft of the rear spar.

A glider tow hook was fitted as standard, as was tail armament of two .5in Browning machine guns in a Boulton Paul D turret. Seven circular windows in each fuselage side and a third dorsal escape hatch were provided.

Production of the A Mk IX ran to 145 machines, all built by Handley Page, the first two examples being delivered in November of 1945. Consequently, Mk IXs soldiered on into the uncertain postwar period, being operated by a handful of squadrons until 1948. In the intervening period they participated in a number of airborne support demonstrations, often in company with Dakotas, air dropping men, guns and equipment, both in the UK and abroad. The A Mk IX equipped No 620 and 644 Squadrons in the Middle East in 1946. Four years later, Egypt purchased six A Mk IXs.

This A Mk IX (RT796) initially served with No 47 Squadron at Fairford and was passed to No 295 Squadron using the same base. (Robertson)

Close-up of the twin Browning tail guns in the D Type turret of the A Mk IX. (M. Wright)

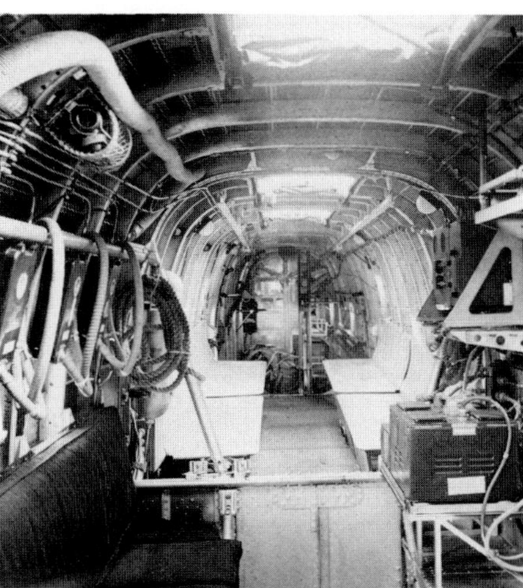

The paratroop seating arrangement of the A Mk IX, looking aft.

Transport Variants

Although postwar Airborne Forces and transport configured Halifaxes invariably took common 'C for cargo' designations as the former role was reduced, the original P. 13/36 specification had considered a transport version as a parallel development and when converted Mk II bombers began to be employed as transports from late 1941, Handley Page put forward three proposals. These were initially known as: Transport A (a stripped Mk III, VI or VII bomber); Transport B (an unarmed version of Transport A); and Transport C, a purpose-built transport (HP 64). In the event, Transports A and B were given priority.

This B Mk III conversion (LV838) served as the prototype C Mk VI, and is fitted with an 8,000lb capacity freight pannier.

Natural metal finish highlights details of an early production C Mk VIII freighter with the freight pannier partially lowered.

C Mk III

First tested with the large freight pannier in 1945, the A Mk III did not fly operationally in this configuration, but emerged as a converted Mk III bomber under the designation C Mk III and incorporating various internal fittings known as Mod 1105, which included locating points for up to nine stretchers or eight passenger seats in addition to rest bunks for the six man crew. Military equipment such as the Monica rear warning radar, flare chute and ammunition tracks were deleted, although the unarmed rear turret was still installed. The dorsal turret location was covered by a fairing and no front gun was fitted. Power plants were Hercules XVIs, as powering the B Mk III bomber.

The first C Mk IIIs were delivered to the Halifax Development Flight of No 246 Squadron in December 1944. The flight was formed to prove the Halifax's usefulness as a transport and became the squadron's 'C' Flight in 1945. No 246 used its Halifaxs for numerous long distance flights to such destinations as Cairo, Iceland and even Moscow.

C Mk VIII (HP 70)

The first mark of Halifax designed from the outset as a transport, the C Mk VIII was based on the Mk VI bomber and was powered by the same engines, Hercules 100s. Mod 1192 gave it the full Transport B fit for the carriage of either ten stretchers, 11 passengers, or freight. The aircraft had a continuous dorsal fuselage section and there was a streamlined fairing in place of the tail turret. The number of circular fuselage windows was increased to eight on each side and the 8,000lb pannier was usually fitted in place of bomb doors. The pannier fitting was covered by Mod 1377 and a special radio fit by Mod 1401.

Serial No PP285 was part of the second production batch of C Mk VIIIs and was retained by Handley Page until March 1948.

Halifax C Mk VIII in the process of transition to civilian duties -- note the crudely applied C-AHYI civil registration. The aircraft was registered to BOAC on 24 September 1946, and used while the carrier's Haltons were being modified. It was returned to the RAF as PP311 on 10 July 1948, its registration then being cancelled.

This C Mk VIII (PP313) also saw civilian service as G-AJPK, initially with Payloads Ltd at Stansted, Essex, then London Aero & Motor Services. It was used briefly a second time by Payloads before being passed to a private charter carrier at Thame, Oxfordshire. (Robertson)

Although almost all C Mk VIIIs left the factory with Green and Grey camouflage over Azure Blue undersides, relatively few actually saw RAF service in these markings. One of those that did was OR A (PP332) of No 301 Squadron, the Polish unit based at Chedburgh for some 15 months (from September 1945 to December 1946), after which it was disbanded. Note the Polish flash carried aft of the small 'AF' code on the nose.

This Halifax A VII (PP350) was the trials aircraft for the 8,300-lb Universal Freight Container. Designed to be dropped at the same time as paratroops, it could carry up to a Jeep and trailer. This March 1951, photo shows the aircraft being readied for a joint US-British exercise at Watchfield, Berkshire, laid on by the School of Land Warfare. (Aeroplane)

The Universal Freight Container was dropped by eight 42-ft diameter parachutes, the first of which can be seen deploying. Underwing cameras to record the behavior of the container as it dropped can be seen under the wings of PP350. (Aeroplane)

Haltons

With a top speed of 320 mph, the C Mk VIII had a range of 2,530 miles and maximum weight was 68,000lbs. The first aircraft (PP225), flew for the first time in June of 1945. Issued initially to five squadrons, the C Mk VIII remained in RAF service until the summer of 1948 when the remaining aircraft were put into storge pending sale or breaking up.

The majority of postwar civilian operated Halifaxes were C Mk VIIIs, 91 receiving British registrations out of a total of 159. The balance was made up by two B Mk IIIs, 32 A Mk IXs and 34 B Mk VIs. The C Mk VIII total included twelve Halton freightliners for BOAC, all of which carried place names beginning with the letter 'F' — Falkirk, Fife, Fremantle and so on.

The Haltons, specially fitted out by Short Brothers of Belfast, could be externally distinguished by larger, rectangular cabin windows, a solid nose fairing which was hinged for baggage loading, and an outward opening cabin door.

BOAC's Haltons served for eighteen months on London-Cairo, Karachi and Accra routes until May of 1948. Sales to private civilian operators were in time for the Berlin airlift which began that August. Seven companies operated forty-one Halifaxes on that historic operation, flying over 8,000 sorties and carrying some 54,000 tons of supplies.

The last of six A Mk IXs supplied to the Egyptian Air Force (EAF) leaving Southend, Essex, on 25 May 1950. Formerly RT907, it was numbered 1162 for the EAF. Its ultimate fate is unknown, but some Halifaxes were destroyed — ironically by Spitfires — during the Suez war of 1956. (Aeroplane)

The Royal Pakistan Air Force was the other non-RAF military customer for postwar Halifaxes, seven B VIs being purchased in 1948. Six of them are seen in this photo, believed to be at Thame, Oxon. At least two aircraft have their RPAF serials visible, that on the far left being Q1279, with Q1277 next to it. An initial letter followed by a three or four digit number was the RPAF's serial identification system. (Aeroplane)

The Empire Radio School at Debden, Essex, had two B Mk VIs, 'Mercury' (RG815) being the second delivered, in July of 1946. Configured as a 'flying classroom', this aircraft had a special navigation radar fit and a modified nose. It made a number of long range flights before being struck off charge in October of 1948. (Aeroplane)

One of BOAC's HP 70 Haltons was G-AHDU 'Falkirk', the prototype for the series. After use by the UK flag carrier, it flew 363 sorties in the Berlin airlift. (BOAC)

One of BOAC's Haltons at Short Brothers' Belfast works in Northern Ireland. Clearly visible are the larger fuselage windows and the port side baggage loading hatch in the nose. (Shorts)

Up she comes. After 30 years underwater, W1048 a B Mk II of No 35 Squadron emerged from the bed of Lake Hoklingen, Norway, on 30 June 1973. (Aeroplane)

'S-Sugar' with members of the RAF sub-aqua team that raised her. The aircraft is now on display at the Bomber Command Museum at Hendon more or less as she was recovered. (Aeroplane)